AF606030

THE QUEEN OF SCOTS – LA REINA DI SCOTIA

THE LORENZO DA PONTE ITALIAN LIBRARY

The Queen of Scots

La Reina di Scotia

FEDERICO DELLA VALLE

Introduction, Translation, and Notes by

FABIO BATTISTA

UNIVERSITY OF TORONTO PRESS
Toronto Buffalo London

Toronto Buffalo London
utorontopress.com
Printed in the U.S.A.

ISBN 978-1-4875-4481-2 (cloth) ISBN 978-1-4875-4510-9 (EPUB)
ISBN 978-1-4875-4529-1 (PDF)

The Lorenzo Da Ponte Italian Library

This volume is published under the aegis and the financial assistance of Agincourt Press Ltd.

Library and Archives Canada Cataloguing in Publication

Title: The Queen of Scots = La reina di Scotia / Federico Della Valle ; introduction, translation, and notes by Fabio Battista.
Other titles: Reina di Scotia. English. | Reina di Scotia
Names: Della Valle, Federico, approximately 1560–1628, author. | Battista, Fabio, translator, editor.
Series: Lorenzo da Ponte Italian library.
Description: Series statement: The Lorenzo da Ponte Italian library | Translation of: Reina di Scotia. | Includes bibliographical references and index.
Identifiers: Canadiana (print) 20220400326 | Canadiana (ebook) 2022040044X | ISBN 9781487544812 (cloth) | ISBN 9781487545109 (EPUB) | ISBN 9781487545291 (PDF)
Subjects: LCSH: Mary, Queen of Scots, 1542–1587 – Drama.
Classification: LCC PQ4621.D24 R4513 2023 | DDC 852/.5–dc23

We wish to acknowledge the land on which the University of Toronto Press operates. This land is the traditional territory of the Wendat, the Anishnaabeg, the Haudenosaunee, the Métis, and the Mississaugas of the Credit First Nation.

University of Toronto Press acknowledges the financial support of the Government of Canada, the Canada Council for the Arts, and the Ontario Arts Council, an agency of the Government of Ontario, for its publishing activities.

Casa Italiana Zerilli - Marimò
New York University

Canada Council for the Arts
Conseil des Arts du Canada

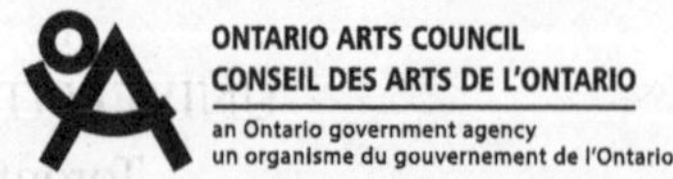

Funded by the Government of Canada
Financé par le gouvernement du Canada
Canada

This book is dedicated to Roberta Donati,
fine conoscitrice di cose stuarde.

Contents

Acknowledgments

I would like to thank Luigi Ballerini and Gianluca Rizzo for enthusiastically welcoming the idea of publishing an English edition of Della Valle's tragedy, and for keenly following its progress. The anonymous reviewers provided valuable suggestions and perspectives that have strengthened the manuscript. Paolo Fasoli, my dear friend and mentor, was instrumental in the inception of this project: his support and words of encouragement helped pave its way, and I am forever indebted to him. Matteo Pace was, as ever, an astute reader and a brilliant companion: it was during a pandemic summer in his Connecticut apartment that much of my translating took place, interspersed with laughter, craft beers, and lobster rolls. My friends and colleagues at the University of Alabama offered advice and feedback on early drafts of the Introduction. I particularly thank Jennie Carr, Matt Feminella, Micah McKay, Alessandra Montalbano, Iñaki Rodeño, and Claudia Romanelli for their comments and support. Jessica Goethals was generous enough to read the entire translation and offer her expert opinion on all aspects of the book: a big debt of gratitude goes to her for her extraordinary patience and graciousness. I would also like to thank Suzanne Rancourt, of the University of Toronto Press, for being unfailingly helpful and precise in her editorial work. Last but not least, my family in Italy followed the development of the book with curiosity, ever reminding me to take care of myself during this long, laborious process.

THE QUEEN OF SCOTS – LA REINA DI SCOTIA

Introduction
From Mary Stuart to Maria Stuarda: Della Valle and the Fictional Afterlives of the Queen of Scots

What little remains of Fotheringhay Castle, in the English Midlands, hardly suggests that it once was the site of one of the most momentous events in early modern European history. Inside the castle's great hall – no longer visible to the contemporary visitor – the unfortunate demise of Mary Stuart, Queen of Scots, came to its gruesome conclusion when, on 8 February 1587, the executioner's axe fell on the anointed sovereign's neck. The spectacle of the execution and the power of its message were not lost on Elizabeth I, Queen of England and Ireland, who had sanctioned it; nor were they lost on its victim, who cleverly opted to reveal a red dress underneath her dark robes once she mounted the scaffold and prepared to die. Red was the colour of martyrdom, and the woman wearing it sent a clear message to the people gathered to witness the gory spectacle and to those beyond the castle that had served as her last prison: Mary would be dying as a martyr-queen, "obedient to what Sacred Rome and its Holy Lord / command and teach" (vv. 2351–2), as Federico Della Valle's character pronounces in *La reina di Scotia* (*The Queen of Scots*). This tragedy, which is presented here for the first time in the English language, was published in 1628 but was composed almost forty years earlier, before 1590: less than three years separated the death of Mary Queen of Scots from its first fictional rendering in a modern vernacular. The modern vernacular in question happened to be the florid Italian of one of Italy's finest tragic poets of the time, Federico Della Valle (ca. 1560–1628). The connection between Mary, her Anglo-Scottish cultural environment, and early modern Italian intellectual history proved to be, as we will see over the coming pages, far from accidental or confined to this specific instance. A retrospective look at Della Valle's *The Queen of Scots* points to this work's centrality in the beginning of a taste, in Counter-Reformation and Baroque Italian literary culture, for a foreign story which lent itself to being reappropriated

and rewritten. Starting with a brief reconstruction of Mary's life, this Introduction will explore key moments in the many fictional afterlives of the queen's story, with a particular – though not exclusive – focus on its Italian dramatic fortune. As a prelude to the tragedy that it presents, as well as to the story itself that it portrays, these introductory pages contextualize *The Queen of Scots* and resituate it as an important stepping stone within a long, varied tradition which spans more than four centuries, from the early modern period to current times.

In the last letter to her maternal cousin Henri, Duke of Guise (24 November 1586), Mary urged him in French, her mother tongue, to persevere in his faith in the rightful cause of Catholicism, defending the honour of the House of Guise: as for her, she wrote, she felt born to shed her blood and offer her body, as Jesus Christ and the martyrs had done, as a voluntary sacrifice to the glory of God.[1] How the daughter of the Scottish king James V and the French noblewoman Mary of Guise went from being the rightful queen of Scotland to contemplating her imminent death at forty-four years of age is a story that both shaped an era and embodied it. Born at Linlithgow on 8 December 1542, Mary was destined to be the only legitimate offspring of James V,[2] who would die of an unknown illness a mere eight days after her birth. The infant, who was crowned queen at nine months of age, soon became the centre of a power struggle between the Protestant king of England, Henry VIII, and the Scottish Catholics, led by Cardinal David Beaton. In 1543, Mary had been promised as the future wife of the English heir Edward, but

1 "May God […] give you the grace to persevere at the service of his Church so long as you live, and may such honour never abandon our race, so that, both as men and women, we may be ready to shed blood to keep alive the cause of our faith […]; and, as far as I'm concerned, I consider myself born, from both my father's and mother's side, to offer my blood for it, and have no intention to give this up. Jesus and all the martyrs who were crucified for us make us, by their intercession, worthy of willingly offering our bodies for his glory" ("Dieu […] vous donne la grâce de persévérer au service de son Église tant que vous viverez, et jamais ne puisse cest honneur sortir de notre race, que, tant hommes que femmes, soyons prompts de respandre notre sang pour maintenir la querelle de la foy, […]; et, quant a moy, je m'estime née, du costé paternel et maternel, pour offrir mon sang en icelle, et je n'ay intention de dégénérer. Jésus crucifié pour nous et tous les saints martyrs nous rendent, par leur intercession, dignes de la volontaire offerte de nos corps à sa gloire." *Lettres, instructions et mémoires de Marie Stuart, Reine d'Écosse*, 6: 464; my translation).

2 James previously fathered two legitimate sons, both of whom died in infancy. He also fathered at least nine illegitimate children, the most influential of whom – not least in the dramatic reception of the story of Mary Queen of Scots – was James Stewart, 1st Earl of Moray, who served as adviser to his half-sister and regent for her son, James VI.

the Scottish Parliament, influenced by Beaton, later rejected the Treaty of Greenwich, which had established the betrothal. Henry VIII thus waged an attack on Scotland, which came to be known as the Rough Wooing, with the aim of restoring the agreement and therefore uniting the two neighbouring countries by marriage. In 1548, months after the death of Henry VIII, the French king Henri II successfully negotiated Mary's engagement with his son, the dauphin Francis. At five years of age, Mary was sent to the French court, only to return to Scotland fourteen years later, in 1561. The intervening years saw her marry Francis, become queen of France in 1559, and finally a widow when her husband unexpectedly died in 1560, shortly after the death of her own mother, Mary of Guise. Upon her return to Scotland, motivated by increasing religious and political tensions, the queen found her country in disarray, threatened by the ever-growing expansionist schemes of neighbouring England, upon whose throne now sat the Protestant daughter of Henry VIII, her second cousin Elizabeth. After the sudden death of Francis II, Mary again became the object of an intense matrimonial strategy, one which, this time, she decided to take into her own hands by marrying her Catholic cousin Henry Stuart, Lord Darnley in 1565. Before doing so, she notably declined Elizabeth's recommendation to marry her Protestant protégé Robert Dudley, Earl of Leicester. By opting to marry Lord Darnley, Mary was ostensibly strengthening her already solid claim to the English throne, which rested upon her being the granddaughter of Margaret Tudor, Henry VIII's eldest sister. Darnley, too, was a grandchild of Margaret Tudor,[3] and it is therefore unsurprising that the marriage between two Catholics boasting Tudor blood and French support raised more than a few concerns in Reformation England, then ruled by a queen whose legitimacy was denied by Catholics.[4] Elizabeth's continuing concerns about Mary's potential designs to overthrow her and seize the English throne appeared to be, after all, not entirely unwarranted. Hostility to Mary, however, was primarily widespread among Scottish lords, and was largely fuelled by her very own treacherous half-brother, James Stewart, Earl of Moray. A particular source of concern became the perceived growing influence over the sovereign of her Italian secretary, Davide Rizzio. Born in the Duchy of Savoy, Rizzio had entered the service of the Archbishop of

3 Darnley's mother, Margaret Douglas, was born to Margaret Tudor and her second husband, Archibald Douglas, Earl of Angus.

4 Elizabeth was Henry VIII's daughter from Anne Boleyn, whose marriage to the king was never recognized by Rome: Pope Clement VII, in fact, had refused to annul the king's previous marriage with the Spanish princess Catherine of Aragon.

Turin as a secretary, before following the ambassador of the Duke of Savoy in Scotland in 1562. There, he was introduced to Mary's court, then leaving his post as an attendant of the Count of Moretta to join the Scottish queen's choir as a bass. A talented singer and lute player, Rizzio gained Mary's trust to the point that she chose him as her personal secretary in 1564. Suspected to be the queen's lover and a spy sent by the pope, Rizzio became the target of a group of conspirators led by Mary's jealous husband Lord Darnley. On the night of 9 March 1566, they burst into the room at Holyrood Palace in which a six-months-pregnant Mary was dining in company that included Rizzio. There, armed with swords, they attacked and dragged him to a nearby room to finish him off. After Rizzio's murder, Mary's relationship with her husband became strained even further, and, despite the welcome birth of a male heir, yet another violent episode was soon to sway the course of events. Less than a year later, on the night of 10 February 1567, after the room where he was sleeping was set ablaze, Lord Darnley was strangled while trying to escape. Suspicion over the queen's responsibility rose quickly, and was ultimately reinforced by her marrying, a mere three months later, James Hepburn, 4th Earl of Bothwell, who was rumoured to be among the conspirators. Whether voluntary or forced,[5] this marriage proved to be the last straw for the Scottish lords who, under the aegis of Moray, were already plotting to overthrow the queen: in July 1567 Mary was forced to abdicate, her infant son James was crowned, and her half-brother became his regent. After several months of imprisonment and a failed attempt to regain power, Mary sought refuge in England, where she was expecting to enjoy the protection of her second cousin Elizabeth. This would prove to be yet another fatal mistake: as soon as she arrived on English soil, she was effectively imprisoned and tried for co-conspiring to murder her second husband. The argument for her guilt largely rested on several forged documents – known as the "casket letters" – allegedly written by Mary to her then-lover Bothwell, attesting to their concerted effort to have Darnley killed. At the end of the trial, Mary was found neither guilty nor innocent. Elizabeth, however, continued to keep her imprisoned until the end of her days. Over a total of nineteen years, Mary was moved to a number of residences, which served as her prisons, and was repeatedly suspected or accused of plotting against Elizabeth's life. One of these attempts became known

5 Despite the efforts of Mary's apologists to argue for her coercion into marriage, the consensus seems to be that, after all, the queen married Bothwell willingly. On this, see John Guy, *My Heart Is My Own: The Life of Mary Queen of Scots* (London: Fourth Estate, 2009), 327–30.

as the Babington Plot, for which she was later tried and found guilty (25 October 1586).[6] Only after nearly four months had passed, however, was her death sentence carried out at Fotheringhay Castle: the widely circulated *Lettera di Sartorio Loschi su la morte de la Reina di Scotia*, which is included in the Appendix to this volume, provides a vivid retelling of the events, and captures the powerful impact that the queen's execution had in early modern Europe. In her letter to Bernardino de Mendoza, the Spanish ambassador to France, written shortly after her death sentence, Mary vividly reaffirmed her self-portrait as a Catholic martyr, as a woman of unerring faith who was about to die under the guise of political wrongdoing but who, in reality, was a pawn in the raging war between orthodoxy and heresy. With uncanny rhetorical foresight, if we consider the remarkable theatrical fortune of her story, she also wrote that she saw workers build her scaffold, for her to "play the final act of the tragedy."[7] Despite these words, however, her tragedy and its legacy had far from reached their final act.

A life such as Mary's was the stuff as fictions are made on, presenting a successful combination of ingredients uniquely suited for a long-lasting literary fortune. Even before her spectacular death on the gallows, the life and demise of the Queen of Scots had become the object of an array of largely nonfictional texts: short chronicles of her birth and her marriages, appearances in larger histories of Scotland and England, and a pervasive presence in diplomatic writings.[8] Several were the defences and narratives of her captivity, among which Francesco Marcaldi's *Narrazione dello stato della Regina di Scotia et del Prencipe suo figliuolo*

6 Devised by Anthony Babington and Jesuit priest John Ballard, the plot aimed to assassinate Elizabeth and put Mary on the English throne, ultimately leading to Catholic restoration. On the Babington Plot, see Guy, *My Heart*, 481–4.

7 "They are at work in my hall; I think it is the scaffold for me to play the final act of the tragedy" ("Ils travaillent dans ma salle; je pense que c'est l'échafaud pour me faire jouer le dernier acte de la tragédie," *Lettres, instructions et mémoires de Marie Start, Reine d'Écosse*, 6: 459; my translation).

8 Public opinion concerning Mary Queen of Scots in the British Isles naturally tended to fall into either attack or praise, along intertwined religious and political lines. Among the most representative earlier works are, on the Catholic side, John Leslie's *A defence of the honour of the right highe, mightye and noble Princesse Marie Quene of Scotlande and dowager of France* (1569) and Adam Blackwood's *Martyre de la royne d'Escosse, douarière de France* (1587), and, on the Protestant side, George Buchanan's *De Maria Scotorum Regina totaque eius contra Regem coniuratione* (1571), soon after translated into English as *Ane Detectioun of the duinges of Marie Quene of Scottes* (1571). On the early reception of Mary Queen of Scots in England, as regarding fact and fiction, see John Staines, *The Tragic Histories of Mary Queen of Scots, 1560–1690: Rhetoric, Passions and Political Literature* (Farnham: Ashgate, 2009).

(1580) enjoyed particularly vast circulation in Italy, including in manuscript form.[9] An anointed queen held against her will by the scheming hands of her English female cousin was already a sensational topic in and of itself, but it was the tragic end of this almost twenty-year-long imprisonment that served as the catalyst for a blooming fortune in fiction. While, as expected, the production of nonfictional narratives also grew exponentially after the events of 1587, it was the flourishing of works of fiction in both verse and prose that sanctioned the entrance of Mary Queen of Scots into the category of *mythos*. And despite examples of sporadic forays into other genres – Bassiano Gatti's heroic poem *Maria regina di Scotia* (1633), for instance[10] – the story of the unfortunate queen was primarily depicted in dramatic works.[11]

1. Mary Queen of Scots and Early Modern Theatre: Della Valle and the First Wave (1589–1628)

In the January 1885 issue of the journal *Rassegna Pugliese di Scienze, Lettere e Arti*, an obscure critic by the name of Gustave Colline discussed two early tragedies on the subject of Mary Queen of Scots. Both shared the same title, *La reina di Scotia*, but one was attributed to Carlo Ruggeri and the other to Federico Della Valle. The two authors were far from popular during the late nineteenth century, as indeed was the person writing about them: behind the French *nom de plume*[12] was a nineteen-year-old aspiring intellectual named Benedetto Croce, who would later become a dominant figure in twentieth-century Italian (and European) aesthetics, politics, and literary criticism. At the time of his writing,

---

9 On Marcaldi, see Brian Richardson, "A Scribal Publisher of Political Information: Francesco Marcaldi," *Italian Studies* 64, no. 2 (2009): 296–313.

10 On this work, and more broadly on the early reception of the Mary Queen of Scots myth in Italy in genres other than tragedy, see Veronica Carta, *Alle origini del mito letterario di Maria Stuarda in Italia* (PhD diss., Università degli Studi di Cagliari, 2011). On the sixteenth-century literary reactions to Mary in England, see James Emerson Phillips, *Images of a Queen: Mary Stuart in Sixteenth-Century Literature* (Berkeley: University of California Press, 1964).

11 To this day, the most comprehensive study on the dramatic fortune of Mary Queen of Scots is Karl Kipka, *Maria Stuart im Drama der Weltliteratur, Vornehmlich des 17. und 18 Jahrhunderts* (Leipzig: Metzler, 1907). For a comprehensive catalogue of poetry, fiction, and music across Europe, see specifically 396–402; for sixteenth- and seventeenth-century theatre, see 403–5.

12 Gustave Colline was one of four main characters in French author Henri Murger's novel *Scènes de la vie de bohème* (1851). Fittingly, Colline was the "philosopher" of the group.

Della Valle's tragedy was already known,[13] but Ruggeri's homonymous work was not. This is why, when introducing it, the critic seized the opportunity to claim Italian primacy over the French in the panorama of the literary reception of the "life of that unfortunate Mary Stuart" ("vita di quella sventurata Maria Stuarda").[14] As a matter of fact, to Croce's knowledge, Ruggeri's *La reina di Scotia* would have predated what was considered to be the earliest tragedy dealing with this subject, Antoine de Montchrestien's *L'Escossaise, ou Le Désastre*, by one year. In reality, however, the French work had already been published in 1601, with the 1605 date to which the critic referred most likely being that of a later reprint, either of the first version or of its revision, which Montchrestien prepared as part of a complete edition of his tragedies in 1604.[15] Despite this erroneous claim, it is true, as Croce would himself discover some time later, that the "birth" of the dramatic Mary Queen of Scots, at least in the vernacular, was indeed owed to an Italian: not Ruggeri, however, but Della Valle. Croce reinforced his somewhat nationalistic argument by bringing into the discussion the figure of a canonical, highly regarded Counter-Reformation intellectual such as philosopher Tommaso Campanella, who, as the critic remarked, had professed to have written a tragedy on the Queen of Scots in the second half of 1598.[16] To Croce's chagrin, the work had gone missing: had it been preserved, he wrote, "we would have *a work of art* on Mary Stuart, written only eleven years after her death" ("noi avremmo *un'opera d'arte* su Maria Stuarda, scritta solo undici anni dopo la sua morte").[17] By assuming that the Calabrian philosopher's tragedy would have been a work of art, the critic was already anticipating his negative aesthetic judgment on Ruggeri's *La reina di Scotia*. Besides the aforementioned problems with chronology, the most outstanding lacuna in Croce's article is represented by his failure to mention – undoubtedly due to a lack of knowledge – what

13 Croce claims having found out about the work – dated 1628 according to its *editio princeps* – by reading an "opuscolo" by Vittorio Imbriani, "ricchissimo di notizie e di curiosità letterarie e bibliografiche di vario genere" ("Notizie di opere letterarie italiane su Maria Stuarda," *Rassegna pugliese di arti e lettere* 2 [September 1885]: 266).

14 Croce, "Notizie di opere letterarie," 266, my translation.

15 This edition of the tragedy would bear the new title *La reine d'Escosse*, by which it is mostly known today. See Jeff Rufo, "*La tragédie politique*: Antonie de Montchrestien's *La Reine d'Escosse* Reconsidered," *Modern Philology* 111, no. 3 (2014), for a recent re-evaluation of Montchrestien's work.

16 During his fifth trial in Naples, Campanella said that he had written the work "per Ispagna contro Inghilterra" (qtd. in Croce, "Notizie di opere letterarie," 267). On Campanella, see also Kipka, *Maria Stuart*, 102–3.

17 Croce, "Notizie di opere letterarie," 267; my emphasis, my translation.

is now considered as the actual first dramatization of the execution of Mary Queen of Scots, one which yet again points to Italy: the five-act *Maria Stuarta Tragoedia*, written in Latin by the French Jesuit Jean de Bordes and staged in Milan's Collegio Braidense in 1589. The drama, which was never printed, was performed just two years after Mary had been executed at Fotheringhay Castle.[18] In the fashion of Jesuit school plays, Bordes' *Maria Stuarta* had a very clear didactic aim, which was to show pupils the capital dangers of heresy and the virtuous conduct of true Catholics.[19] Since the play itself was written in Latin, the teacher had deemed it necessary to provide summaries of each act in Italian so that his audience might have better understood it, not without showing some impatience at his pupils' subpar skills in the classical language. A Frenchman writing in Latin and Italian for a Milanese public school about an Anglo-Scottish subject is itself an immediate indication of the inherent transnationalism of the Queen of Scots story. As he states in the prologue (also in Italian), his retroactive decision to add vernacular synopses to the Latin play had come as a consequence of the complaints he had received for his use of "a peregrine, strange language" ("lingua peregrina, e strana").[20] This linguistic attention to the understanding of the message, and the choice of a contemporary story, rather than a biblical one, are two elements that draw attention, very early on, to the reputation of the Queen of Scots and the potentialities of her story. A mere two years after her death, Mary had already gained the status of a Catholic martyr, worthy of being included in the canon passed on to the younger generation. The exemplary quality of her sacrifice is at the core of Bordes' dramatic intentions, as it will be in the works produced after it, despite their not sharing any direct ties to it. In fact, the influence of the *Maria Stuarta Tragoedia* was virtually nonexistent. Rather than giving birth to a dramatic tradition, Bordes' work remained what it was meant to be: a circumscribed, aim-specific play that was conceived as part of an educational curriculum. Most of the Catholic propagandistic

---

18 The manuscript (MA0022) is preserved at the Morgan Library & Museum in New York City. It was purchased in 1906 by Pierpont Morgan from London's J. Pearson & Co. and is arguably the most important literary piece in the library's Mary Stuart Collection, which was assembled between 1906 and 1912.

19 Four years after Bordes, another French Jesuit schoolmaster, Adrian Roulers, published his *Stuarta Tragoedia* (Douai: Officina Typographica Viduae Boscardi, 1593), which he had conceived for his pupils to perform. On Roulers, see Kipka, *Maria Stuart*, 94–102; on the Jesuits and their educational use of theatre, see Giovanna Zanlonghi, *Teatri di formazione: Actio, parola e immagine nella scena gesuitica del Sei-Settecento a Milano* (Milan: Vita e Pensiero, 2002).

20 Bordes 2r.

elements that would become central throughout the literary fortune of the Queen of Scots are already present in this play: Mary's innocence, her unwavering faith, her victimization, the greed of others, the Christological symbolism of her death on the scaffold. But because it never went into print, the *Maria Stuarda Tragoedia* remained an obscure witness to the event at Fotheringhay that, in a matter of two years, would be the subject of its first vernacular dramatization.

In a review of what he considered to be the oldest of the Italian tragedies on the Queen of Scots, Croce gave a brutally – and hilariously – frank assessment of its literary quality. Carlo Ruggeri's *La reina di Scotia* (five acts, in verse) received a much more negative evaluation than Della Valle's, anticipating the reviewer's appreciation for this latter work, which would spark the rediscovery itself of the Piedmontese author. Ruggeri's tragedy was deemed abysmal: in his very curt account of its background, Croce wished that this *Reina* were not only the first, but also the last of Ruggeri's dramatic efforts.[21] Very little is known about the author, who was likely from the Naples area. The tragedy was printed in that city by Costantino Vitale in 1604, and was likely never staged. As Croce argued, Ruggeri's one-dimensional portrayal of Mary proposed her as "only a victim of Protestantism, a martyr of Catholicism" ("soltanto la vittima del protestantesimo, la martire del cattolicesimo"),[22] leaving out "womanly" qualities that, as we will see, would ultimately be highlighted in the later dramatic production.

Today, however, we know that the first major dramatic contribution in the Italian language to the subject of Mary Queen of Scots is the work of Federico Della Valle. Little is known about Della Valle's life; he was likely born in the vicinity of Asti, in the Duchy of Savoy, to a middle-class family. He was employed at the Savoy court, which is confirmed by an epithalamium he wrote in 1585 for the wedding of Charles Emmanuel I and the Spanish infanta Catherine of Austria, daughter of Philip II of Spain.[23] After authoring a number of panegyrical poems for his patron Charles Emmanuel,[24] Della Valle staged the tragicomedy *Adelonda di Frigia* at the

21 See Croce, "Notizie di opere letterarie," 267.

22 Croce, "Notizie di opere letterarie," 267.

23 See Giovanna Romei, "Della Valle, Federico," in *Dizionario Biografico degli Italiani*, vol. 37 (Rome: Istituto della Enciclopedia Italiana, 1989), and Carlo Filosa, "Contributo allo studio della biografia di Federico Della Valle," *Giornale storico della letteratura italiana* 17 (1938): 161–210. See also Matteo Durante, "Per una biografia culturale," in Federico Della Valle, *Opere*, vol. 1, ed. Matteo Durante (Messina: Sicania, 2005), 8. For a broad monographic study of the author and his works, see Franco Croce, *Federico Della Valle* (Florence: La Nuova Italia, 1965).

24 See Durante, "Per una biografia culturale," 8–10.

court in 1595.[25] After this effort, however, Della Valle's employment at court appears to end: already at the beginning of the year, as we will see, he had dedicated the second draft of his tragedy on Mary Queen of Scots to Ranuccio Farnese, Duke of Parma and Piacenza, and around 1599 he was looking for the patronage of Filippo d'Este, Marquis of San Martino in Rio.[26] Between 1603 and 1606, he was in Spain with Charles Emmanuel's elder sons, and then in Milan after 1621.[27] In this very year, Della Valle wrote an oration dedicated to Philip IV of Spain on the occasion of his father's funeral. In 1627 he oversaw the printed editions of his biblical tragedies *Ester* and *Iudit*, which had both been composed between 1590 and 1600;[28] the following year, shortly before or after his death (1628), his masterpiece *The Queen of Scots* was printed in Milan by the heirs of Melchior Malatesta, with no record of it ever being performed on stage. The tragedy, composed in *endecasillabi* and *settenari* with no precise rhyme scheme,[29] presents no internal division into acts and scenes.[30] By the time of its printed publication, more than forty years had passed since Mary's execution. The textual history of Della Valle's tragedy, however, goes back almost the same number of years. Besides the 1628 *editio princeps*, in fact, Della Valle's work is transmitted by two manuscripts: one, preserved in the Naples National Library, was uncovered by Benedetto Croce in 1936, fifty years after he authored the article quoted above;[31] another, preserved in the Bergamo Civic Library, was made known by Bruno Baldis in 1952.[32] Despite, as Matteo Durante claims, not being an autograph,[33] the Bergamo

25 See Durante, "Per una biografia culturale," 20–1.

26 See Romei, "Della Valle."

27 See Romei, "Della Valle."

28 On Della Valle's three tragedies, see Franco Croce, *Federico Della Valle*, and Laura Sanguineti White, *Dal detto alla figura: Le tragedie di Federico Della Valle* (Florence: Olschki, 1992).

29 *Endecasillabi* are verses with the main stress on the tenth syllable, by far the most used in Italian poetry, while *settenari* are verses with the main stress on the sixth syllable.

30 Durante interprets this absence as Della Valle's adhesion to the sixteenth-century Italian modernization of the legacy of classical tragedy ("La Maria Stuarda dellavalliana," 350n).

31 See Croce, "Ancora della *Reina di Scotia* di Federigo Della Valle," *La critica* 34 (1936). The autograph manuscript that Croce found in the Naples National Library is entitled *Maria la reina*.

32 On this, see Bruno Baldis, "Di una nuova redazione manoscritta della tragedia *La Reina di Scotia* di Federico Della Valle," *Aevum* 26 (1952): 349–64. Also this manuscript bears the title *Maria la reina*.

33 For a detailed and very convincing philological analysis of the Bergamo manuscript vis-à-vis the Naples manuscript see Matteo Durante, "La prima redazione della *Reina di Scotia* di Federico Della Valle (Bergamo, Biblioteca Civica, ms. MM166 [S III 24])." Matteo Durante, *Restauri dellavalliani* (Catania: Università di Catania, 1983), 9–59, and "La Maria Stuarda dellavalliana," in *In assenza del re. Le reggenti dal XIV al XVII secolo*, ed. Franca Varallo *(Piemonte ed Europa)* (Florence: Olschki, 2008).

manuscript appears to be the older of the two. While the Neapolitan manuscript found by Croce (and signed by Della Valle) bears a dedicatory epistle to Ranuccio Farnese, which is dated 1 January 1595, the Bergamo manuscript features a different dedicatory epistle, this time addressed to noblewoman Vittoria Solara and dated 1 January 1591. We may therefore take this date to be the *terminus ante quem* in reconstructing the drafting of Della Valle's work. The tragedy was thus conceived not long after the execution of the Queen of Scots, bearing further evidence to the immediate resonance of the event outside the British Isles, and especially on Catholic soil. As Della Valle claims in the first dedication to Vittoria Solara, it was she who had prompted him to write a tragedy about the life and death of Mary Queen of Scots, which had to have been completed sometime in 1590.[34] Already from the first manuscript version to the second, the author conducted substantial revisions on both the linguistic and, understandably, the rhetorical levels, eliminating overtly encomiastic references to the Savoia family.[35] In the much later printed edition, Della Valle's revisions achieved the result of streamlining the dramatic action, further emphasizing the centrality of Mary as the undisputed protagonist, and thus eliciting strong anti-Protestant reactions in his readers. That Della Valle was a fervent advocate of Counter-Reformation spirituality with close ties to Turin's Jesuitic intellectual circles cannot, and should not, be denied.[36] But to read *The Queen of Scots* as just an anti-Protestant manifesto does not do justice, I believe, to the argumentative complexity of the work. While the religious theme is ostensibly central, to the point of lending itself to a typological reading, the ensuing analysis of the text will concentrate on the sparse, crystallized dramatic action to highlight the technique employed by Della Valle in his construction of the martyr-queen character. This technique rests on the reversed mirroring of Mary's qualities onto the defects of Elizabeth, which is conducted more by implying rather than showing.

If the dedicatory epistles included in the Bergamo and Naples manuscripts appear to be the most traditional, in their being addressed to

34 See Durante, "Per una biografia culturale," 13–14.

35 See Durante, "La Maria Stuarda dellavalliana," 348.

36 On the subject of Jesuits and their influence on dramatic performance in seventeenth-century northern Italy, see Annamaria Cascetta and Roberta Carpani, eds., *La scena della gloria: Drammaturgia e spettacolo a Milano in età spagnola* (Milan: Vita e pensiero, 1995). Specifically on the relation between Della Valle's work and Jesuit tragedy, see Cesare Colombo, "Federico Della Valle a Milano," *Italia Medioevale e Umanistica* 9 (1966): 477–85, and Roberto Mercuri, "La *Reina di Scotia* di Federico della Valle e la forma della tragedia gesuitica," *Calibano* 4 (1979): 142–61.

noble patrons, the third dedication, which opens the 1628 printed edition, is a different matter. Addressed to Pope Urban VIII, born Maffeo Barberini (1568–1644), this epistle is both the most concise among the three and the most historically relevant: the pope, in fact, was no stranger to the subject of Della Valle's tragedy, and had himself contributed to Mary's early literary canonization.[37] In the wake of the death of the Scottish queen, young Maffeo Barberini had written an epitaph – read by Della Valle in George Conn's biographical *Vita Mariae Stuartae Scotiae Reginae, dotariae Galliae Angliae ac Hiberniae Heredis* (1624)[38] – lamenting her tragic fate and celebrating the merits of the queen. Roughly forty years after its conception, *Maria la Regina* – as it is entitled in both manuscript versions – was ready to be embraced by someone who had personally been touched by the tragic event, and to assume its new, geo-specific title.

Della Valle's portrayal of the Queen of Scots during the final hours of her imprisonment, to which I will come back later, displays what will become a consolidated technique throughout the rest of the dramas devoted to what Croce defined "the Maria Stuarda theme."[39] Mary is inherently characterized as the holy, virtuous half of a whole, whose other evil, sinful half is inhabited by Elizabeth: to talk of Mary meant to talk of Elizabeth. The peculiarity of Della Valle's technique, however, is the representation *in absentia* of the Queen of England: evoked, hinted at, even named, but never present.[40] If Mary is flesh and soul, Elizabeth is a haunting shadow. The physical absence of the antagonist is in stark contrast to Bordes' *Maria Stuarta Tragoedia,* in which the Queen of England is very much present and active, in a way that is similar to the later dramatic production of the 1660s and 1670s. Besides reinforcing the distance between Della Valle's creation and Bordes', this dramatic choice also appears to be historically accurate. Famously, the two queens were cousins and rivals who probably never met in person: their interactions were carried out exclusively in writing or

37 Just one year before, Spanish playwright Lope de Vega had published – and also dedicated to the pope himself – the *Corona trágica: Vida y muerte de la serenísima reina de Escocia María Estuarda* (1627). For a modern edition, see Lope de Vega, *Corona trágica: Vida y muerte de la serenísima reina de Escocia María Estuarda,* ed. Antonio Carreño-Rodríguez and Antonio Carreño (Madrid: Cátedra, 2014).

38 The epitaph ("Te quamquam immeritam ferit, o Regina, securis") is an opening paratext in Conn's work (Rome: Ioannes Paulus Gellius, 1624; Würtzburg: Stephanus Fleischmann, 1624).

39 Croce, "Il tema Maria Stuarda," 84.

40 On this aspect, see also Sanguineti White, *Dal detto alla figura*), 29–30.

through emissaries.[41] Moreover, the visual removal of Elizabeth from the dramatic action served both aesthetic and ideological purposes. The first reference to Elizabeth in *La reina di Scotia* relies on a mechanism of mirroring through omission, which makes the unfortunate state of the Queen of Scots the visible consequence of an invisible scheming designed by her unseen, and as of yet unnamed, rival:

How darkly and cruelly
did you move, oh sun, on that day when the impious shores,
the impious shores and deceitful, heinous sands
of England did my unhappy feet touch,
which brought me there as a queen
with crown and honours,
but with the fate of a servant,
abducted and chained!

Deh, come oscuro e crudo
rotasti, o sol, quel dì che l'empio lido,
empio lido e spergiura infame arena,
d'Inghilterra toccò l'infausto piede,
che me portò con nome di reina
coronata, onorata,
e con destin di serva
rapita, catenata! (vv. 51–8)

Mary, who is pictured here, as indeed throughout the tragedy, as lamenting her condition and awaiting death, blames her setting foot in England as the starting point to her sorrows. But England is almost a metonymy, insofar as it coincides with the person who governs it and who had determined her fate as a captive woman. Ten lines later, Elizabeth's name makes her entrance into the drama through the words of her very rival, when Mary refers to her first through the synecdoche "tyrannical hand" ("mano tiranna") and then as "impious enemy" ("empia […] nemica," v. 72). The extreme density of these two phrases captures the spirit of Della Valle's style throughout the work: bare bones, essential, evocative. Elizabeth is presented as an enemy who is tyrannical and ungodly,

41 The bibliography regarding the relationship between Mary and Elizabeth is immense. Besides the most recent biographical works by John Guy (*My Heart Is My Own* and *Elizabeth*, respectively), a very good analysis of the fatal collapse of the two queens' rapport is Jayne Elizabeth Lewis, *The Trial of Mary Queen of Scots: A Brief History with Documents* (New York: Bedford/St. Martin's Press, 1999).

the two features that were, and would continue to be, unfailingly associated with her figure in Catholic propagandistic discourse. The political and the religious are conjoined here, the one serving as reason and explanation for the other: her heretical nature is expressed by her role as a ruthless usurper, and vice versa. The materially invisible presence of Elizabeth in the play manages to obtain a twofold, seemingly contradictory, result. On the one hand, it intensifies the centrality of Mary, who is the sole, rightful protagonist in her path to martyrdom. On the other, it makes Elizabeth speak more loudly, and appear more daunting, than if she had been an acting, visible *dramatis persona*. Among the numerous instances in which the Queen of England is either directly mentioned or the indirect protagonist of narrative passages, by detractors and partisans alike, two deserve particular attention. Probably the most consequential in terms of *actio* is the favourable portrayal offered by the Counsellor Beale, whom she has sent to Mary to make her (ultimately deceptive) demands known to her prisoner. This figure is ostensibly based on Robert Beale, Clerk of the Privy Council, who historically was entrusted with reading the death sentence to the Queen of Scots, and subsequently with writing the official report of her execution.[42] Elizabeth is, in his words, a noble queen, one who, even without acquitting her, is moved by the tribulations endured by her cousin:

My queen, moved by pain
for your misery, where you were brought
by your fault of wanting too much,
and by your obstinate, false opinions,
by which you took thousands and thousands of souls to the deepest abyss
of eternal darkness, sends me here.

La mia regina, mossa da l'affanno
de le miserie tue, dove t'addusse
colpa di voler troppo, et ostinata
e falsa opinion, onde traevi
teco mill'alme e mille ai ciechi abissi
de le tenebre eterne, a te mi manda. (vv. 868–73)

In the emissary's words, the Queen of Scots is thus the victim of her own greed and deceptive conviction of being the rightful heir to the

42 For an extensive study of the role played by Beale in this circumstance, see Patricia Basing, "Robert Beale and the Queen of Scots," *British Library Journal* 20, no. 1 (1994).

English throne, echoing the very same accusations levelled at Elizabeth by her anti-Protestant detractors. But what is most poignant in the Counsellor's speech is the following section, in which he delineates his queen's requests with the supposed aim of subverting the death sentence and stopping an execution that was already inevitable. Elizabeth demands that Mary renounce her claim to the throne of England, that she give up her very title of queen in favour of her son James,[43] and that she abide by the laws of the Royal Council. But after these more strictly political conditions, the Counsellor moves to the real centrepiece, the matter of religion:

> She then wants you
> to confirm the past things
> done in Scotland, which were introduced
> there by the new religion and the new worship
> [...] and promise
> for yourself, your son, and the kingdom
> that they will be observed entirely.
> [...] and let Rome be declared impious and fallacious
> for centuries to come to the Scottish kings
> and people, and to Scotland as a whole.
>
> [...]. Poscia vuol anco
> che tu confermi le passate cose
> in Scozia fatte, e già colà introdotte
> con nuova religione e nuovo culto
> [...], promettendo
> tu, per te, per tuo figlio e per lo regno,
> ch'osservate saranno illese, intatte.
> [...] E si pronunzi Roma empia e fallace,
> nei secoli avenir, ai re scozzesi,
> ai popoli, a le genti, a Scozia tutta. (vv. 885–902)

The other, opposite, portrayal of the English queen is provided deep in the dramatic action by the Butler. A faithful servant of his mistress, the Queen of Scots, the man – a one-dimensional "mask," like most of the secondary characters in this tragedy – launches an actual invective against God, in

43 As a matter of fact, as we have seen, Mary had already been forced to abdicate in favour of her then-infant son on 24 July 1567, twenty years prior to the time in which Della Valle's tragedy should be set. See Introduction, p. 6.

the style of Job, which is acceptable to the reader because it pleads Mary's case. Lamenting the inscrutable workings of his divine plan ("you rule over human things and throw / spears of reward and punishment for our actions" / "volvi le cose umane, e premi e pene / libri con lance a le nostr'opre eguale," vv. 1662–3), the Butler then addresses his desperate anger towards the Queen of England, a monster-like "head" ("testa," v. 1669), who seems to rise above God and mortals alike:

And on the other side, the haughty head
rises and merges with clouds
and wants, and demands, and obtains,
and speaks, and commands, and rules over right and wrong
with a firm and proud hand,
over what is unjust and impious, and disposes of other people's
wills and lives by her own will.

E d'altra parte sorge,
e con le nubi mesce
l'altèra testa, e vuole, e chiama, e impetra,
e dice, e impera, e volge il dritto e 'l torto
con man superba e forte,
l'ingiusto e l'empio, e come di sua voglia
fa de la vita e de la voglia altrui. (vv. 1669–75)

Della Valle's skilful use of polysyndeton (through the repetition of the conjunction "and") is here at its most effective. The dehumanized, hydra-like figure of the unnamed queen is characterized not only by her mingling with threatening natural elements such as the clouds, but by the incessant, pounding list of verbs that describe her all-encompassing, tyrannical behaviour: the repeated use of the conjunction "and" creates both a pressing rhythm that reflects the ticking time of Mary's execution, and totalizes the discrete units of the speech into an insurmountable whole.

As expected, the characterization of Mary moves along opposite lines: that Della Valle's aim is to portray the Queen of Scots as a Catholic martyr is both evident and successfully achieved. By the end of the tragedy, she becomes an actual sacrificial lamb, even mimicking the posture of Christ in accepting her fate. Before leaving her chamber for the last time, Mary, in the Butler's testimony, stares at the crucifix hanging above her bed, moves towards it "with open arms" ("con le braccia aperte," v. 1752) and kisses it ardently: the open arms, here, perfectly mirror Christ's, but while in this latter instance the opening is forced

by the nails on the cross, in the former it is a voluntary act. But Mary, as I suggested earlier, is not only a symbol of Catholicism and martyrdom: she is also a queen whose life story is familiar to Della Valle. This story's canonization of resistance rests both on her Christological portrayal and on her "human" qualities. In fact, the strength of Della Valle's approach is in the overlapping of these coexisting aspects.

The 1628 *editio princeps* features the addition of a prologue, harking back to the canonical structure of Greek tragedy, in the form of a lengthy monologue spoken by the Shade of the King of France (the queen's first husband, Francis II). This at times thundering lamentation provides basic background information and sets the tone for Mary's imminent first appearance. The queen's opening lines articulate a self-portrait that will echo almost incessantly throughout the tragedy, becoming a veritable leitmotif:

> Behold me, who was once a queen
> with two illustrious crowns and sceptres,
> which at once ruled over French and Scots:
> daughter of a king, wife of a mighty king,
> descended from a long line of kings,
> and mother to a king.
>
> Rimiri me, che già reina adorna
> di duo chiare corone e di duo scettri,
> che resser ad un tempo Franchi e Scoti,
> figlia di re, moglie di re possente,
> discesa per lungo ordine da regi,
> e di re madre ancóra, […] (vv. 8–13)

Besides proudly claiming her (past) sovereignty over France and Scotland, she then proceeds to illustrate her royal persona: daughter and descendant of kings, wife of a king, mother of a king. This ternary identity embraces her past, her present, and her future, strengthening the argument that establishes her as the sole, real queen in the story, and assimilating her womanly nature (daughter, wife, mother) with the sacredness of queenship. This tripartition is designed as an obvious blow to Elizabeth, who is neither wife nor mother, nor, according to her detractors, rightful descendant of kings because of her illegitimate birth. But the use of this self-portraying technique – relying on the divine number three – contradicts, I believe, the commonly held view of Mary as resigned to the inevitability of her death. On the contrary, in the early stages of the tragedy, the Queen of Scots is still struggling to

come to terms with the fact that she will soon die, which is signalled by her reliance on her genealogical self-portrait. In her first monologue, Mary reiterates it three times. The first we have just seen, the second is articulated in the negative, the third goes back to the positive of the first one. This oscillation suggests a thought process that begins with a resolute affirmation, continues with the crisis of the affirmation, and then regains the optimistic stance of the opening. The middle point, which is the lowest, is articulated by Mary as follows:

Captive queen,
disconsolate widow, abandoned
mother of a useless son,
mistress of a rebellious, treacherous people,
woman without counsel,
destitute, ill, of decaying age.

Reina prigioniera,
vedova sconsolata, abbandonata
madre d'inutil figlio,
signora di rubella infida gente,
donna senza consiglio,
povera, inferma et in età cadente. (vv. 39–44)

The positions of status that previously served as sources of pride have been upended: her royal lineage has brought her to be the queen of an unworthy people, her marriage has resulted in widowhood, her maternity has produced a useless son. But by the end of her monologue, the order is restored by repetition:

[…] Yet I was born,
I was born the daughter of a king, and the heiress
of an ancient kingdom;
I was the wife of a glorious king, and the mother
of a king, who from me inherits
mantle and sceptre and crown;

[…] dunque nacqui,
nacqui figlia di re, fui poscia erede
d'antichissimo regno,
d'eccelso re fui moglie, e son madre anco
di re, che da me prende
manto e scettro e corona; (vv. 59–64)

By this insistence on her ternary nature, we see the Queen of Scots as fundamentally unable to come to terms with her demise. Even though she describes herself as a wretched prisoner, she still retains a fragment of hope which rests upon the exceptionality of her sacred nature. Through obsessive repetition, not only does she remind herself of that nature, but she implies – again using a technique of reverse mirroring – that Elizabeth cannot harm her more than she already has over the course of "twenty unhappy years" ("vent'anni infelici," v. 30). And despite the images of martyrdom that Della Valle employs right from the start,[44] Mary still has not fully accepted the sacrifice that comes with her martyr role. She fantasizes an escape, and the theme of hope is even the subject of the chorus that follows the arrival of a servant who brings news of the possibility that Elizabeth may either change her mind or forced to do so. And when hope, though ephemeral, seems to become more tangible, Mary's fantasy immediately goes back to the gloriousness of her nature – rooted in the Scottish land – almost using it to legitimize the rightfulness of hope itself:

Oh, that I could
see again the fields
of my beloved homeland,
of the kingdom where the long, ancient stream
of my glorious blood
ran amid sceptres and crowns;
where the ashes lie
of the many noble bones
which gave flesh to my tired flesh!

Oh, se fia mai ch'io giunga
a riveder i campi
de la mia patria amata,
del regno, ove già lungo antico rivo
del sangue mio ben glorïoso corse
fra scettri e fra corone;
ove 'l cenere giace
di tant'ossa onorate,
ond'ebber carne queste carni stanche! (vv. 805–13)

44 Among other instances: "My victory will be in burial!" ("Mia vittoria sarà la sepoltura!" v. 178); "[…] for me, I believe, / heaven stopped its workings and stands still, / perhaps looking at what a wretched, / abandoned woman at last will do" ("[…] per me il cielo / cessa, or credo, da l'opre fermo stassi, / forse a mirar quel che farà alfin donna / misera abbandonata," vv. 246–9).

The real turning point in the tragedy is represented by the crucial moment, already mentioned above, of Beale's exposition of Elizabeth's demands: Mary's response is, as expected, a complete rejection of her rival's will, and determines her final assumption of the robes of martyrdom in its purest etymological meaning, that of a witness of faith. She refuses giving up her title, using divine right as her justification;[45] she renews her natural claim to the English throne but leaves it to the people's will to decide whether she is wanted or not; and lastly, she proves unwilling to negotiate her faith, either personally or for her subjects. The whole argument, in each of its three points, is rooted in her unerring faith in the divine plan, and, by refusing with the utmost strength the last of Elizabeth's demands, she implicitly gives further legitimacy to the rejection of the previous two. Her profession of Catholic faith substantiates both her claim to martyrdom and the abandonment of all hope:

> or that I consent that it take sacred orders and rites
> from anywhere other than the Roman seat,
> is an impious demand,
> and the hope that I will accept it is foolish.
> And if my refusal has to be paid
> with blood, here is my blood, and here is my throat.
> I am not so bound to this life
> or kingdom that I should desire one or the other
> tainted by impiety!
>
> o ch'io consenta ch'egli prenda altronde,
> fuor che del roman seggio, ordini e riti
> nei sacri uffici, è empia la dimanda
> e sciocca la speranza d'impetrarla.
> E se 'l mio contradir ha da pagarsi
> col sangue, eccoti 'l sangue, ecco la gola.
> Non sì amica son io di questa vita,
> o del regno, ch'io brami o l'una o l'altro
> con l'impietà congiunta! (vv. 948–56)

45 "I must not and will not take away from myself / what *God gave me*. He, in his mercy, / made me be born a queen: in dying, / He shall receive me as a queen. *May the royal / sign follow my unbound soul*" ("Tôrre a me stessa quel che *Dio mi diede*, / né 'l debbo, né 'l consento. Ei, sua mercede / nascer mi fe' reina: anco reina / mi riceva morendo. *Il regio segno / segua l'anima sciolta*," vv. 923–7; my emphasis).

Mary finally acknowledges the artificiality of Elizabeth's move and the cruelty of her nature ("an enemy once, but now she keeps me for her amusement"; / "nemica un tempo, or m'ha per scherzo," v. 1056), which allows her to relinquish her earthly expectations and fix her eyes on her life after death, a death that she will make exemplary. As in mystical discourse, the Queen of Scots accepts her humbling designed by God,[46] but agency, as displayed in the masterfully orchestrated scene of her death, never ceases to be hers and hers only: the exceptionality of her nature makes her, until the very end, witness, judge, and defendant (vv. 1353–4).[47] The very figure of resistance, she confirms her sentence as fair, but only in view of the imminent, now deliberate acceptance of her sacrificial fate: it is her adamant, obstinate refusal of Protestantism that gives her the power to look eagerly towards her demise, as a martyr would.

The pronouncing of the death sentence is entrusted, in *La reina di Scotia*, not to Beale, but to the Earl of Cumberland, a character based on George Clifford, who participated in the trial of the Queen of Scots. The entire procedure is quite complex, and introduces a death scene that, through pauses and accelerations, takes up more than one thousand lines (of a total 2635). The sentence is written by Elizabeth, partly read by Mary herself – the lines concerning the mode of death – read aloud by Cumberland. The promise of Mary's freedom is articulated, in Elizabeth's writing, in the expression of the end of her physical life and the pretended, sardonic continuation of her spiritual life:

> The path to your freedom is a hard one,
> but still useful and straight. – Let this head
> be detached from the neck, and let the soul
> fly where it must, and go freely:
> this is allowed to it. –
>
> La via di liberarti è dura via,
> ma pur utile e dritta. – Si discioglia
> dal collo quella testa, e l'alma voli
> poi dove deve, e 'n libertà se 'n vada,
> ché ciò le si concede. – (vv. 1426–30)

46 "Let my fate / have this too: I thank God, / who likes to humble me. I will wait for them here, / since I am here" ("Si concede / questo anco a la mia sorte, e grazie a Dio, / cui piace umiliarmi. Io qui gli aspetto, / poiché qui sono; […]," vv. 1262–5).

47 It bears pointing out that Mary, under great duress, uses the masculine forms of these words.

The most striking feature of the death sentence is, of course, the punchline: the Queen of England *allows* the soul of the Queen of Scots to go freely wherever it may. Through a written reported speech, Elizabeth intervenes here in the dramatic action, restating her power and dominance over her captive cousin. And Mary, as usual, is quick to capture this cruel and unusual detail and to turn it against her invisible enemy by bringing back the genealogical discourse of blood, this time, however, involving Elizabeth herself. The lines "to me, whose blood I am / of the blood whence she was born" ("á me, che sangue sono / del sangue ond'ella nacque," vv. 1443–4) inaugurate a preoccupation with the theme of kinship, which, until this moment, had been quite marginal. Mary exploits the discourse of family relation in order to not only lament her condition but to further demonize her evil counterpart: Elizabeth is a cruel woman to whom she is heir,[48] and even more poignantly, the relationship between the two is "from woman to woman, / from queen to queen, / from niece to aunt" ("donna a donna, / e reina a reina, / a la zia la nipote," vv. 1480–2). In this way, the dehumanization of the unseen Queen of England is complete, as a prelude to Mary's sacrificial ending. And in order to strengthen her argument, Mary here acknowledges her rival as a peer in queenship ("from queen to queen"), only to go back to her usual stance a few lines later, when she claims her innocence in the supposed plot against Elizabeth and blames her own awareness of illegitimacy as the sole impetus: "Her own faults, / believe me, make your queen fear, / not my deceits or tricks" ("Il proprio fallo, / credimi, fa temer la tua reina, / non arte, o insidia mia," vv. 1549–51).

The final moments in the life of the Queen of Scots are marked, as I already suggested, by a dilation of time, which serves to showcase Mary's embracing of martyrdom. The execution per se takes place – conventionally and expectedly offstage – between lines 1974 and 1979, its notice entrusted to the Chorus, who does not see it, but rather *feels* it through its internal senses: "It's done, it's done! / The cruel blow was stricken, / I felt it in my soul. / She is no more, my queen is no more: / she left me, she departed!" ("[…] È fatto, è fatto! / Fatto è 'l colpo crudele, / l'ho sentito ne l'alma. / Non è più, non è più la mia reina. / M'ha lasciato, è partita!" vv. 1975–9). The complex mechanism devised by Della Valle, however, does not signify the Queen's reported passing as the be-all and end-all of the dramatic action: rather than the climax, death is but the instrument that allows Mary's figure to continue speaking and to be seen post mortem, through her own words and those of others, in an

48 Mary both regarded Elizabeth as a usurper and considered herself her rightful heir.

effort to emphasize both her holiness and the unending power of her body politic. Mary again stresses her ternary nature: "Mistress by nature, / your mother by affection, / your companion by fate" ("Padrona per natura, / ma per affetto madre, / per sorte compagna," vv. 1906–8), as she describes herself right before leaving the stage to be executed. This time she speaks not in genealogical terms, but rather in relation to her loyal subjects: the divinely designed mistress, on the one hand, and the mother/partner, on the other.[49] And Mary's exceptionality is again reinforced by her words of affection for her Lady-in-Waiting, reported by the Butler, in which she emphasizes her image as an immortal queen and a mortal woman coexisting in the same body: "[...] how dearly / she held her *queen*, / she held her *Mary*" ("per quanto cara / ebbe la sua *reina*, / ebbe la sua *Maria*," vv. 2115–17, my emphasis).

Mary's last self-identification, nearing the very end of the dramatic action, is again entrusted to the Butler and is a lengthy speech that encompasses all the key themes in her story, becoming in effect a manifesto not only of Della Valle's tragedy but of the mainstream Italian reception of the Queen of Scots. First, it restates the dual opposition with her rival Elizabeth; then it proceeds to deny all fault regarding the attempted treason with which she is charged; and lastly, it proclaims her unwavering Catholic faith. The most noteworthy aspects in this final reported speech have to do with the first and last of the points that I just outlined. When reflecting on her enemy, Mary goes back to her previous ternary formulation to illustrate her relationship with Elizabeth, who is again referred to as woman, queen, and aunt,[50] but emphasizing her cruelty by claiming innocence and affection.[51] Building on this rhetorical attack on her opponent and affirmation of guiltlessness, her final words gain even further effectiveness and give us her ultimate self-portrait:

> Thus, I die happy. If there is among you
> someone who shares the same feeling,
> I beg you pray for me and in any place

49 The Chorus will later return to this image: "Oh, sweet care / from the sweetest, most beloved *queen*, / how you sharpen my anguish / by showing me the *dear, maternal* affection / of a lost *mistress*!" ("Ahi, dolce cura / di *reina* dolcissima et amata, / come inacerbi in me, lassa, l'affanno, / con mostrarmi *materno* e *caro* affetto / di *padrona* perduta!" vv. 2195–9; my emphasis).

50 "a woman who believes a woman, / [...], / and a queen who believes a queen, / [...], / and a niece who believes an aunt" ("donna che crede a donna, / [...] / e reina a reina / [...] / e nepote che crede ad una zia," vv. 2297–301).

51 "whom she never offended, but always / loved and honoured" ("non offesa giamai, ma sempre amata / et onorata sempre. [...]," vv. 2302–3).

and any time bear witness
that Mary Stuart dies a queen,
obedient to what sacred Rome and its holy Lord
command and teach.
I am ready to die.

Così moro ben lieta. Voi, s'alcuno
v'è pur fra voi ch'abbia il medesmo senso,
prego preghi per me, e 'n ogni luogo,
in ogni tempo, testimonio renda
che Marïa Stüarda muor reina,
ubidïente a quell ch'impera e insegna
Roma sacrata et il Signor suo santo.
Et eccomi a morire. (vv. 2346–53)

This is the third time that the Queen of Scots is named, and the only one in which she is self-naming – albeit through the Butler's mediation – with the addition of the name of her House, a moment that is emphasized by the two diereses that metrically elongate it, giving it more weight. Complemented by the vivid description of her fair flesh and beautiful neck being pierced by the deadly axe, leaving a "trembling corpse, whence blood rushed out / in great gushes" ("cadavero tremante, onde si sgorga / per grosse canne il sangue," vv. 2434–5) which still cannot take anything away from the gracefulness of her mouth, the martyr-queen is finally born.

2. Mary Queen of Scots and Early Modern Theatre: The Second Wave (1663–1672)

After the early efforts by Bordes, Della Valle, and Ruggeri – conceived in the wake of Mary's execution – the interest in the story of the Queen of Scots in Italy came to a halt until the 1660s. As a possible explanation to both this hiatus and the resurgence of the story, historian Stefano Villani has argued that the renewed "explosion of the theme of Mary Queen of Scots in Italian literature [...] must be linked to news of the Restoration of the Stuarts in 1660."[52] After the execution (1649) of Mary's grandson, Charles I, the culmination of what came to be known as the English

52 Stefano Villani, "From Mary Queen of Scots to the Scottish Capuchins: Scotland as a Symbol of Protestant Persecution in Seventeenth-Century Italian Literature," *Innes Review* 64, no. 2 (2013): 113.

Revolution, and the ten-year parenthesis of the Interregnum under the leadership of Puritan radical Oliver Cromwell, the reinstatement (1660) of Charles II as legitimate king was received with some enthusiasm in Catholic Italy. Though officially a Protestant, Charles II was rumoured to be a crypto-Catholic, and showed a favourable disposition towards Catholicism in general.[53] If the first wave of Italian dramatic works was prompted by the spectacular death of the Catholic queen, the second wave may well have resorted to her then-canonized image as a way of, yet again, voicing hope for a Catholic restoration. From a literary viewpoint, however, these later dramatic works appear to be uninterested in the religious subject, or rather, they use its repository of images, themes, and topoi but empty it of the Catholic spirit that permeates the earlier works. As we will see, while still remaining the narrative climax, Mary's martyrdom is no longer viewed as the "perfect example" presented by Della Valle and Ruggeri: the war between orthodoxy and heresy is an inevitable ingredient in the dramatic rewritings, but it is no longer the most important one. The story of the Queen of Scots is tackled with a large degree of ideological freedom: the great-grandmother of the then-current king of England had by the 1660s reached a mythical status that allowed her to be "employed" in a number of different ways.

Five tragedies based on the story of Mary Queen of Scots were published in Italy between 1663 and 1672: *Maria Stuarda* by Giovanni Francesco Savaro (three acts, in prose; 1663), *La barbarie del caso*, by Domenico Gisberti (three acts, in verse; 1664); *La Maria Stuarda regina di Scotia e d'Inghilterra*, by Orazio Celli (three acts, in prose; 1665); *I trionfi di morte*, by Antonio Paccinelli (five acts, in prose; 1670); and *Maria Stuarda*, by Anselmo Sansone (three acts, in verse; 1672). With the partial exception of Paccinelli's tragedy, on which I will focus later, these works share much affinity, due to their common debt to an earlier French tragedy by Charles Regnault, *Marie Stuard, reyne d'Écosse*, which was first performed in 1637 and printed in 1639.[54] The dramatization of the last days of the Queen of Scots as presented in this work and in its Italian re-elaborations shifts the emphasis to different dynamics and storylines, producing different results. We can identify, in addition to the theme of unrequited love introduced by Regnault, the fading of the

---

53 On the subject, see Ronald Hutton, *Charles II: King of England, Scotland, and Ireland* (Oxford: Oxford University Press, 1990).

54 Another dramatic work concerning the queen written around the same decades is *Mary Stuart, or Tortured Majesty*, by Joost van den Vondel (1646). For a modern edition, see Joost van den Vondel, *Mary Stuart, or Tortured Majesty*, ed. Kristiaan P.G. Aercke (Ottawa: Dovehouse, 1999).

subject of martyrdom into an empty rhetorical exercise which rests on the common knowledge of the queen's demise, and finally the rise to prominence of a political fight fuelled by the stronger narrative roles of Mary's half-brother, the Earl of Moray, and Elizabeth.

As suggested above, Regnault's *Marie Stuard* brings an element into the story of the Queen of Scots which had been ignored by Della Valle and Ruggeri: a "marriage plot" involving the Duke of Norfolk, Thomas Howard (1538–1572). The storyline is, at least broadly speaking, historically accurate. Under the influence of Secretary of State William Maitland, Mary had embarked upon the idea of marrying Norfolk (1569),[55] a union that, as John Guy argues, could potentially have been beneficial to both parties, since "Mary would use the marriage to seek her restoration as the Queen of Scots, and Norfolk would use it to assert his claim in right of his wife to the throne of England."[56] Elizabeth, however, became enraged when she was made aware of this scheme, and had Norfolk imprisoned in the Tower of London, putting an end to the plan. As we can already see from this brief outline, such a plot provided a perfect occasion to bring a fully fledged love triangle to the forefront of the Queen of Scots story, adding an as yet unprecedented layer of contrast between the two queens: Mary and Elizabeth are now seen as rivals not only in matters of religion and state, but also of love. Although this device is first introduced in Regnault's tragedy, the French playwright still essentially applies it to the theme of martyrdom:[57] as Alexander S.

55 Mary, however, was still married to Bothwell. This is why she planned on asking the pope for annulment, by virtue of the ceremony having been conducted within the Protestant rites. Despite having met Norfolk only once, Mary engaged in a thick exchange of passionate love letters with the English nobleman, partly in accordance with the conventions of royal courtship, partly denoting her desperate attempts at securing the duke's affection and consequently a prospect of freedom (see Guy, *My Heart*, 461–2).

56 Guy, *My Heart*, 462.

57 The reference model, for Regnault, is *La reyne d'Escosse* (1601–4) by Antonie de Montchrestien, which canonized the literary image of Mary as a martyr in France. Towards the end of the tragedy, Montchrestien's Mary launches a fully fledged martyrological invective against those who are killing her, in a way that is close to the many lamentations of Ruggeri's coeval *Reina di Scotia*: "Ie mourray pour sa gloire en defendant ma foy. / Ie conqueste une Palme en ce honteux supplice, / où ie fay de ma vie à son nom sacrifice, / qui sera célebré en langues divers; / une seule couronne en la terre ie perds, / pour en posséder deux en l'éternel Empire, / la couronne de vie, et celle du Martyre" (124; "I will die for his glory in defence of my faith. / I earn a palm in this shameful supplice, / whereby I make my life a sacrifice to his name, / which will be celebrated in different languages; / only one crown on earth do I lose, / to acquire two in the eternal empire, / the crown of life, and that of martyrdom"; my translation). What is most interesting in this passage is the recognition and anticipation of the myth-making surrounding the parable of Mary.

Wilkinson argues, "the enduring portrait of Mary as a tragic Catholic figure was to be the legacy of her own performance on the scaffold at Fotheringhay."[58] But by the mid-1660s, more than twenty-five years after Regnault's work was conceived, the Italian dramatists were playing with a legacy both historical and literary, and exploring argumentative potentialities that were already contained in the very subject treated. As Villani remarks, "events surrounding the Queen of Scots were now more than seventy years old" and all authors writing on the subject had been born after Mary's death.[59] The martyr-queen, Rome's sacrificial lamb against the transgressions of heresy, had lost the original significance of her symbolic message, or rather had become a tool for discussion on a broader range of topics.

The earliest of the 1660s Italian dramas, Savaro's *Maria Stuarda*, was printed in Bologna in 1663. The son of a sailor, Savaro was the archdeacon of Mileto, in Calabria,[60] until he moved to Rome, where he became a member of the Accademia degli Umoristi, and then to Bologna, in whose university he was appointed professor of rhetoric.[61] He was a prolific writer, in genres ranging from satire to local history, oratory, and tragedy. Interestingly, Savaro also wrote another English-themed tragedy, *Anna Bolena*, which was staged also in 1663 and printed the following year. Of all the Italian authors of Mary Queen of Scots tragedies, Savaro was the only one who displayed a broader interest in Tudor and Stuart affairs. This is also attested by printer Giacomo Monti in his preface to *Anna Bolena*, where he claimed that the stories of the English royals had replaced those of the Greek House of Pelops as a repository of subjects for tragedies.[62] *La barbarie del caso* by Gisberti was first performed on the Venetian island of Murano in 1664, and printed later in the same year by Francesco Valvasense, the renowned printer of

58 Alexander Wilkinson, *Mary Queen of Scots and French Public Opinion, 1542–1600* (New York: Palgrave Macmillan, 2004), 159.

59 Villani, "From Mary," 113–14.

60 An interesting side note regarding this geographical area is that Gregorio Panzani (1592–1660), who was bishop of Mileto – and therefore Savaro's direct superior – from 1640 until his death in 1660, had served as papal legate to Queen Henrietta Maria (and Charles I, ostensibly) in 1634. Venetian ambassador Angelo Correr describes his mission in detail (329–30). For more information about the figure of Panzani, see Stefano Villani, "Panzani, Gregorio," *Dizionario Biografico degli Italiani*, vol. 81 (Rome: Istituto della Enciclopedia Italiana, 2014).

61 *Archivio storico della Calabria*, vol. 1, no. 3 (Cosenza: Pellegrini, 2012), 50.

62 On the fictional fortune of Anne Boleyn's story, see Stephanie Russo, *The Afterlife of Anne Boleyn: Representations of Anne Boleyn in Fiction and on the Screen* (New York: Palgrave Macmillan, 2020).

the Incogniti.[63] Gisberti's work was accompanied in at least five scenes by a musical score composed by Pietro Molinari. The rest of the tragedy would appear to have been recited, rather than sung.[64] The whole production of the play, sponsored by the Accademia degli Angustiati, of which Gisberti was a member, seems to have been quite grandiose: seven radical changes of scene, two major dances, four stage machines, including one that would make a pageboy appear to magically fly (a Venetian Ariel, almost) and one that would create waves from which dancing nymphs arose. Unlike the sombre atmospheres depicted by Della Valle and Ruggeri, this was clearly meant to be a spectacle, and the financial investment in it must have been substantial. Very different is *La Maria Stuarda, regina di Scotia e d'Inghilterra*, by Celli, which saw the light in 1665, just one year after *La barbarie del caso*. This tragedy was staged[65] and printed in Rome by Michele Ercole, a printer who seemed to display a more canonical taste than Valvasense, having just produced an edition of Battista Guarini's pastoral tragicomedy *Il pastor fido*, which also included the *Rime* by the same author, as well as Tasso's *Aminta*. Also of note in Celli's work is the dedication, which is to Prince Camillo Pamphili (1622–1666), ex-cardinal,[66] nephew of Pope Innocent X (born Giovanni Battista Pamphili, 1574–1655), and son of the infamous "Pimpaccia," Olimpia Maidalchini (1591–1657). Celli, moreover, cites some of his sources, declaring in the preamble that the tragedy was "gathered from the history written by Father Caussin" ("dedotta dall'istoria

63 Valvasense's history is a troubled one. Tightly associated with the group of "libertine" intellectuals that orbited around Venetian aristocrat Giovanni Francesco Loredan (1607–1661), whose often scandalous books he printed, Valvasense was brought to trial by the Venetian Holy Office in 1648, after his bookshop had been raided and was found ridden with "heretical" books (including some by Ferrante Pallavicino, as well as *Adone* by Giovan Battista Marino). On 4 February 1649 the printer was sentenced to recanting and imprisonment, after a month of which he was let out on house arrest and given licence to resume his trade. For a thorough reconstruction of the Valvasense trial and its context, see Mario Infelise, *I padroni dei libri: Il controllo sulla stampa nella prima età moderna* (Rome-Bari: Laterza, 2014). For the relationship between the Incogniti and England, see Stefano Villani, "Gli Incogniti e l'Inghilterra," in Davide Conrieri, ed., *Gli Incogniti e l'Europa* (Bologna: Emil di Odoya, 2011): 233–76.

64 The Library of Congress, which has a digitally reproduced, free-access copy of the printed edition, actually qualifies *La barbarie del caso* as a "libretto."

65 It was performed during the Carnival celebrations in Palazzo Pamphili. On this, see Saverio Franchi, *Drammaturgia romana: Repertorio bibliografico cronologico dei testi drammatici pubblicati a Roma e nel Lazio, Secolo XVII* (Rome: Edizioni di Storia e Letteratura, 1988), 388.

66 He left religious life in 1647 to marry Olimpia Aldobrandini and continue the Pamphili line.

descritta da P. Causino"), that is, the immensely popular section on Mary Queen of Scots from Nicolas Caussin's *La cour saincte* (1638), which was also translated into Italian by Carlo Antonio Berardi in 1648.[67] Lastly, *La Maria Stuarda* by Sansone, an Olivetan monk from Mazara del Vallo, was published in Palermo by Pietro dell'Isola in 1672. The frontispiece identifies Sansone as the "true author of *Geneviefa*" ("vero autore della *Geneviefa*"), which, as we find out in the author's notice to the reader, is a tragedy that he had written ten years prior but that had been published four years earlier by someone else.[68] The Sicilian monk, too, cites his sources: Nicholas Sanders, Giacomo Bosio, Nicolas Caussin, Hilarion de Coste, and Florimond de Raemon.[69] Indeed these four dramatic works geographically encompass the whole of the Italian peninsula, from Bologna and Venice, through Rome, to Palermo, offering further proof of the wide traction of the myth of the Queen of Scots.

These late tragedies engage the theme of martyrdom in a way that is both limited and rhetorical. The Queen of Scots has become a multifaceted woman by the 1660s, and although works produced in a Catholic context cannot set aside the religious struggle, the introduction of the romantic storylines gives us a less hagiographical perspective. What is interesting to note here is that the emphasis on love is accompanied by an even greater emphasis on politics. Savaro's *Maria Stuarda* clearly places Mary in the middle of a power struggle for the control of Scotland and England, conducted by way of secret betrothals, betrayed promises, and attempted marriages. Gisberti's *La barbarie del caso* is the first Italian tragedy to explicitly engage with Mary's life after the death of her second husband, Lord Darnley. We have seen that Della Valle

67 The work is the *Histoire de l'incomparable Reine Marie Stuart, Reine de France et d'Escosse*, published as part of *La cour sainte* (Paris: Chappelet, 1624). The Italian Jesuit Berardi translated it as *Historia di Maria Stuarda, Regina di Francia e di Scotia* (Bologna: Carlo Zenero, 1648).

68 Sansone must have referred to *La Geneviefa, o sia l'innocenza riconosciuta*, indeed printed by the already mentioned Giacomo Monti in Bologna in 1668 and attributed to Girolamo Abbati.

69 Besides the already mentioned works by Sanders and Caussin, Sansone's other two references are to less influential works: historian Florimond de Raemon's (1540–1601) posthumous *Histoire de la naissance, progrès, et décadence de l'hérésie de ce siècle* (1605), and friar and biographer Hilarion de Coste's (1595–1661) *Eloges et Vies des reynes, princesses, dames et damoiselles illustres en Piété, Courage et Doctrine, qui ont fleury de nostre temps, et du temps de nos pères* (1630). The reference to Giacomo Bosio (1544–1627) is more obscure: the historian mentions Mary Queen of Scots in his *Historia della sacra religione et illustrissima militia di San Giovanni Gierosolimitano* (1589; 761), but this is a very brief and ultimately uniformative passage, hardly enough to provide material for a dramatic rewriting.

stops at Francis II – the Shade of the King of France in *La reina di Scotia* – while Ruggeri jumps from Darnley to the death sentence. Gisberti, on the contrary, openly addresses what was in fact one of the biggest problems in Mary's biography, especially among Catholics: her marriage to Bothwell. Widely regarded as responsible for Darnley's death in 1567, Bothwell would soon after become Mary's third and last husband, with the marriage taking place in a Protestant ceremony.[70] The most influential, pro-Protestant account of these events was provided by Scottish humanist George Buchanan in *Ane Detectioun of the duinges of Marie Quene of Scottes* (1571), in which he "exposed" the queen's supposed treachery and collusion with Bothwell in the murder of Darnley. Having been essentially hired by the Earl of Moray to build a case against his half-sister, the credibility of Buchanan's *Detectioun* was questionable from the start, as critics have widely pointed out: John Guy has argued that Buchanan "was distorting the known facts to create an interpretation of reality of almost complete fantasy,"[71] and Tricia McElroy has brought attention to the text's successful rhetorical strategies, including the creation of "the illusion of an open legal hearing in which the reading audience assumes an adjudicatory role."[72] Buchanan's work is referenced – but not endorsed – in *La barbarie del caso*, in lines spoken by the evil Moray as a way of arguing for Mary's guilt in Darnley's assassination.[73] In reconstructing Mary's life from her birth to her final imprisonment at Fotheringhay, Gisberti clearly identifies Moray as chiefly responsible for the queen's misfortunes: a sort of Iago who plots and schemes unseen, he sides with Elizabeth in order to quench his thirst for power and exact vengeance against his half-sister. Although the three acts of *La barbarie del caso* are a chaotic, confused, and often excruciatingly contradictory cauldron of subplots, disguises, *anagnorises*, and sudden deaths,[74] it is nonetheless clear that

70 For a detailed reconstruction of events, including the controversial kidnapping and supposed rape of the queen, see Guy, *My Heart*, 328–35.

71 Guy, *My Heart*, 391.

72 Tricia McElroy, "Performance, Print, and Politics in George Buchanan's *Ane Detectioun of the duinges of Marie Quene of Scottes*," in Caroline Erskine and Roger A. Mason, eds., *George Buchanan: Political Thought in Early Modern Britain and Europe* (Farnham: Ashgate, 2012), 50.

73 Gisberti, *La barbarie del caso*, 53.

74 Benedetto Croce declared that he would have summarized its action "if it were not so very lengthy and if summarizing it were not impossible; besides, such an act would make its comic nature dissipate" ("se non fosse lunghissima, e il riassumerla quasi impossibile e tale, per giunta che, riassumendola, tutto il comico sfumerebbe," "Notizie di opere letterarie," 310).

Moray is behind every machination, and is eventually punished for his evil deeds.[75] The same holds true for the works by Celli and Sansone, reinforcing the ties between these later tragedies and the detachment from the subject of Catholic martyrdom. Celli has Moray declare his nefarious intentions openly, while Sansone displays some originality by having Moray already dead in pre-diegetic time and having him intervene in the tragedy in the form of a shade. Mary refers to her half-brother's greed for power at the very beginning of the play, and then proceeds to portray herself as gullible for having fallen for Moray's treachery. It is significant that Mary is self-described as a simple woman who can be tricked into believing things she should not, a trait that is also evidenced by Celli with the same language. The reputation of the Queen of Scots appears to have undergone a makeover in 1660s and early 1670s dramas. Mary's betrayed trust had always been a central point in her literary and historiographical portrayal, but the late tragedies propose a different outlook: what is at stake here is not the innocence of a devout Catholic but the weakness of a woman. By enlarging the dramatic action, moving the spotlight away from the individuality and exemplarity of Mary's path to martyrdom as a witness of Catholic faith, the later authors shift the focus to a different set of interests and connections, not least of which is the tie between carnal desire and political power. If Mary is a simpleton, Elizabeth is a temptress, a "daring Alcina," as Sansone defines her,[76] who is riding the wave of Moray's treacherous plans in order to satisfy her own needs to eliminate the Queen of Scots. After all, these later tragedies emphasize a fundamental distinction between the two women that had thus far been sidelined for the sake of the religious argument: there is no question that Elizabeth is a much more skilled politician than Mary. If the strength of the Queen of Scots relied on her saintlike figure, once the exemplarity of faith is no longer the exclusive focus of the dramatic action, the character loses her strength. But while Elizabeth's early demonization as a Protestant is supplanted by a watered-down, commonplace idea of reason of state,[77] Mary's holiness does not find an apt replacement: as Savaro's portrayal suggests, she is only a weak

75 In Gisberti's tragedy, Moray is killed by Mary's son James (143), who had been disguised as one Amiltone, only to reveal his identity at the beginning of act 3 after an awkward "love scene" involving himself and Elizabeth disguised as his mother.

76 Sansone, *Maria Stuarda*, 68.

77 The "knowledge of the means suitable for founding, maintaining, and enlarging a State," to quote Friedrich Meinecke, *Machiavellism: The Doctrine of* Raison d'état *and Its Place in Modern History* (Boulder: Westview, 1984), 67.

woman, neither saint nor queen, trapped in a game that she is unable to either understand or handle. To Elizabeth's programmatic acknowledgment that a sovereign must be like the many-eyed giant Argus in Celli's drama, Mary indirectly replies with the well-known narrative of her misfortunes and her falling prey to the evil designs of others.[78] Of the four authors, Celli is the one who provides the best explanation of this shift in argumentative dynamics by having Elizabeth explain her reasons to Mary in Machiavellian terms: she claims that her actions are dictated by necessity ("necessità") and not by choice ("eletione"),[79] providing a stark contrast to the helplessness of the politically naïve Mary. It is therefore most natural that the scheming, state-conscious ruler Elizabeth should become associated with the obscure puppet master Moray, both motivated by their quest for power and by their shared background as bastard children.[80] These four late works on the Queen of Scots, therefore, share the same interest in the humanization of characters, with a close attention to the dynamics of statecraft. The tragic grandeur that Della Valle had bestowed upon the solitary figure of a queen that would break but not bend is completely lost in these later reworkings of her myth. The very death of Mary is deprived of its Christological symbolism because it does not come as the direct, inevitable consequence of the dramatic action: it is only a stereotyped side note, something that readers and viewers who, by then well acquainted with the main lines of the story, had come to expect. The moral strength and spiritual integrity of the Queen of Scots are so unimportant that, in *La barbarie del caso,* Gisberti omits (or forgets) having Elizabeth's demands include her cousin's religious conversion to Protestantism, a demand which, in earlier works, embodied the very motor of the tragic action. The dignity of Mary's death, traditionally consigned to a third-person narration, becomes an occasion for Senecan gore in Sansone's version, where the beheading takes place on stage. The exemplarity of the queen's sacrifice is transposed to a dimension of theatrical entertainment; but although it could still teach by showing it did not elicit catharsis.

Among the tragedies on Mary Queen of Scots published in this period, the one that stands out for its originality is *I trionfi di morte,* written by Antonio Paccinelli, from Arezzo, and printed in Perugia in 1670. However little known the author is today, his work is even less known: as a

78 Celli, *La Maria Stuarda,* 8.
79 Celli, *La Maria Stuarda,* 39–40.
80 Gisberti, *Al barbarie del caso,* 40.

matter of fact, I uncovered this tragedy in September 2018.[81] The main claim to originality in this five-act prose drama rests upon the insertion, within the narrative of the demise of Mary Queen of Scots, of the brutal assassination of Davide Rizzio, who appears as a *dramatis persona*. Although he does not provide any specific indication regarding his sources, Paccinelli hints at an "erudite pen" ("erudita penna") that had already recorded the tragic fate of the Queen of Scots: the reference is likely to the French Jesuit Nicolas Caussin, whose history of Mary Queen of Scots (from *La cour sainte*) enjoyed immense success and boasted several translations. The influence, if not the knowledge, of the previous tragedies by Gisberti, Celli, and Savaro is close to non-existent: besides the original presence of the Rizzio subplot, the narrative of Paccinelli's work is unrelated to the other works, largely because the secondary romantic plots of Norfolk and Leicester are almost entirely absent. In *I trionfi di morte* we see Mary in her married life, as queen, lover, and wife: the action revolves around her last two husbands – Darnley and Bothwell – and condenses a very long chronology (more than twenty years) into a convoluted dramatic plot, expectedly culminating in the queen's beheading, narrated by a witness (the governor of London). In this version of the story, Mary is not yet imprisoned by Elizabeth, but trapped into a loveless marriage to the jealous Bothwell ("Feraspe, conte di Botuello"), whom her half brother Moray ("Armidoro Conte di Moravia Fratello naturale di Maria") had compelled her to marry after the death in battle of her beloved Lord Darnley[82] ("Henrico Stuardo Conte di Lenox sotto nome d'Alvante consigliero"). As a matter of fact, Darnley is very much alive, only having feigned death,[83] and now, unrecognized by anyone, is back at court to win her over. After Darnley makes his identity known, Bothwell engages in a struggle for Mary's heart, which ends with his

81 The copy I consulted is at the Morgan Library & Museum in New York, where it is preserved as a part of the Mary Stuart Collection, assembled in the early twentieth century. Other copies of the book are preserved at the Universitätsbibliothek Leipzig, the New York Public Library, the Biblioteca Città di Arezzo, the Bibliothèque Nationale de France in Paris, and the Biblioteca Nazionale Centrale in Rome.

82 Interestingly, at the time of his alleged death, in this version of the tragedy Darnley is not yet married to Mary. This is why Bothwell is indeed presented as the queen's second husband, rather than her third, thus making the ensuing union with Darnley – which, incidentally, is made possible while she was still married to Bothwell by virtue of the violence that she had suffered at the hands of the man – the last one. By the end of the tragedy, Mary will die his widow, rather than Bothwell's. Her son James, who is referred to as a boy, is presented as the offspring of her first marriage, to Francis II.

83 One of the innumerable blind spots and inconsistencies in *I trionfi di morte* has to do with the reason why Darnley chose to pass as a victim of war, which is never addressed, let alone given an explanation.

being expelled from court and in the new marriage between the queen and his rival. Meanwhile, the scheming Moray orchestrates Darnley's violent death, and persuades Elizabeth (who never appears on the scene) that Mary has plotted against her with the Duke of Norfolk (who also never appears). This brings us to Mary's execution, but not before Moray's own demise.[84] In this intricate, confused storyline, the inclusion of Rizzio would not only appear as unexpected but as unnecessary. The Italian secretary, however, is given arguably the most important role in the overall narrative: as the queen's chief adviser, he functions as an analyst, a third-party observer who works as both a political "theoretician" and a chronicler. In a court where the principal actors are concerned with the dynamics of love and power, Rizzio is the flag bearer of *ragion di stato*. Far from the ambitious courtier depicted by Buchanan, this Italian secretary speaks only on behalf of Mary's interests as they overlap with those of the state. The most important function bestowed upon Rizzio in *I trionfi di morte* is that of opposing Mary's reunion with Darnley in matrimony, a stance that will prove fatal for him: also in the narrative of this play, it is to Darnley's violence that the secretary falls victim. The insertion of the Rizzio episode within the narrative of *I trionfi di morte* directs the attention towards the interplay between the interests of love and the interests of the state. By playing with the portrait of the Italian secretary coming from the historiographical tradition and canonized by Caussin, Paccinelli gives us the image of a true servant of politics, whose loyalty to the queen and her welfare is rewarded with death. And it is precisely this aspect of Rizzio's character that sheds light on the Queen of Scots' own shortcomings as a ruler. By the end of the tragedy, Mary's death is above all else the demonstration of her inability to rule according to the safe principles of a seasoned statesman such as Rizzio: although many of the traditional images of martyrdom are still present, it is nonetheless clear that this tragedy's focus is far removed from Catholic apology. More than any of the other authors of Mary Queen of Scots tragedies, Paccinelli does not shy away from Mary's mistakes, but rather engages with them in a critique of her nature as a woman.

3. An Undying Myth: From Theatre to Opera and Beyond

After the seventeenth century, the myth of Mary Queen of Scots in fiction experienced several important resurgences in different genres and media. The pervasiveness of this story is so profound that it would be

84 He is killed by gunshot by one of Mary's faithful men.

almost impossible to present a complete summary account into these final pages; rather, the focus will remain on the works that are the most relevant to the perspective of performance, especially, where possible, those relating to Italian culture.[85] With the exception of the tragedy *Maria Stuarda* (1778) by the celebrated Romantic poet and dramatist – not to mention, Della Valle's fellow townsman – Vittorio Alfieri,[86] the later Italian fortune of the Queen of Scots' story became inextricably tied to melodrama, which surged as a "national" phenomenon throughout the nineteenth century. Between 1813 and 1895, sixteen operas on this subject were composed, twelve of them either first staged in Italy or authored by Italians and premiering abroad.[87] A substantial number of these operas, including the one which today is by far the most famous, Gaetano Donizetti's *Maria Stuarda* (1834), take their origins from Friedrich Schiller's tragic masterpiece, *Maria Stuart* (1800). It was the work of the German playwright that ultimately fuelled the myth of Mary Queen of Scots in nineteenth-century Europe and beyond, giving us a version of the story that complements, and expands, some of the thematic developments of the earlier dramatic work.

Vittorio Alfieri famously disavowed his five-act *Maria Stuarda* and regretted having written it. It is not hard to see that, when compared to his later masterpieces, such as the tragedies *Saul* (1782) and *Mirra* (1784–6), the earlier work clearly stands out as less refined and lacking the distinctiveness and incisiveness of the poet's more mature language. Nevertheless, Alfieri's *Maria Stuarda* is an important step in the modern treatment of the Queen of Scots, even more so because it does not focus its dramatic action on the conventionally explored last days of her life. In fact, Alfieri depicts a moment that, as we have seen, dramatists had largely steered clear of, that is, the circumstances that led to the end of Darnley's life and to Mary's marriage with Bothwell. *Maria Stuarda*, however, stops short of the third, damning marriage, confining the action to the queen's discovery of her second husband's assassination. The other characters in the play are Arrigo (Darnley),

85 For a thorough inventory of eighteenth- and nineteenth-century European drama, see Kipka, *Maria Stuart*, 403–13.

86 A few other tragedies were also composed during the nineteenth century, including *Il trionfo dei Carbonari* (1802) by the much less-known dramatist Camillo Federici, which was the source of Luigi Carlini's opera *Maria Stuarda, regina di Scozia* (1818).

87 These figures come from Stella Rollet, "Les princes martyrs, héros d'opéra au XIXe siècle: Le cas de Marie Stuart," in *Le sang des princes: Cultes et mémoires des souverains suppliciés, XVIe–XXIe siècle*, ed. Paul Chopelin and Sylvène Édouard (Rennes: Presses Universitaires de Rennes, 2014), 211–25.

Lamorre (Moray), Ormondo (Elizabeth's emissary), and Botuello (Bothwell). The dramatic action begins with Mary voicing her anger towards Arrigo for his role in the murder of Davide Rizzio, whom she describes as a lowly foreigner, despite his having acquired considerable power at court. Because of his role in the Italian's death, Arrigo had been shunned. The action revolves around a supposed plot that would have Arrigo and Ormondo kidnap Mary's son in order to bring him to England, where Elizabeth would have him raised as a Protestant. Ormondo makes the queen believe that the plan had been devised by her own husband, and she responds by having Botuello surround Arrigo's residence with his troops. Lamorre disapproves of this decision and predicts both Arrigo's assassination and Mary's own, to which she reacts by begging him to save her husband. Botuello, however, announces that no one is allowed inside Arrigo's castle. Meanwhile, an explosion is heard and Lamorre declares that Arrigo's dead body is among the building's ruins: the tragedy closes on Mary's cry for vengeance. Even from this brief outline, we can see that Alfieri's queen is essentially portrayed as somewhat fickle, even impressionable. As she states herself, not without some facetiousness, in her first exchange with Arrigo (act 2, scene 3), she is young, naïve, and weak because she is a woman. Throughout the play, her actions are unfailingly dictated by others, and perhaps it is not surprising that all the other *dramatis personae* are men: from start to finish, Alfieri shows us a woman who has neither the tragic grandeur of Della Valle's Mary nor and the vitality of the other seventeenth-century versions of her, haphazard and chaotic though they may be. Conversely, the character who is closest to a tragic hero is Arrigo, a man whose fatal *hybris* determines his demise. Even the queen's final vow of vengeance comes off as stiff and unconvincing, especially given her half-brother's damning prediction shortly before.

The contrast with Schiller's *Maria Stuart*, composed some twenty years later, could not be greater. To begin with, it dramatizes the final hours of the queen's life and gives an impressively substantial role to Elizabeth, who is presented as a well-rounded co-protagonist in the action. Historical facts are altered in order to fit dramatic needs, most notably to showcase what is by far the best-constructed confrontation scene between the two rival sovereigns in the entire canon (something that Donizetti would be more than ready to seize upon for his own opera). Schiller's other noteworthy invention is the character of Mortimer, the nephew of Mary's jailer Amias Paulet, who reveals himself to be a fellow Catholic working to set her free. The queen is imprisoned by Elizabeth because of her responsibility – which she does not deny – in Darnley's murder: the real reason behind her imprisonment, however, is her claim to the English throne. Elizabeth is still hesitant

about signing the death warrant, which keeps Mary's hopes of freedom alive. After a long period of waiting, the queens finally meet, and the encounter ends with a bitter argument because Mary does not accept Elizabeth's demands. Meanwhile, Mortimer has both tried to get Leicester to help Mary and attempted to let her escape: when this is found out, Mortimer commits suicide and Leicester distances himself. After this, Elizabeth signs the death warrant, citing the will of the English people as motive. The death warrant finally arrives in the hands of Elizabeth's prime minister, Lord Burghley, who acts upon it by having Mary executed. The English queen blames Burghley and her other men for carrying out the death sentence and is eventually left alone as the tragedy comes to an end. Through the juxtaposition of Elizabeth's skilled pragmatism and Mary's tragic idealism, Schiller, as a number of critics have noted,[88] used the story to showcase his concept of the sublime, one of the cornerstones of his philosophical thinking.[89] The Scottish queen is turned into a beautiful young woman – a deliberate historical inaccuracy and a stark contrast to Della Valle's depiction of an old, ailing monarch – whose courage in enduring the ultimate trial of death is the very mark of her sublimity, of her ability to transcend the human, embodied by Elizabeth's political machinations. Setting aside the refinement of Schiller's philosophical framework, it is nonetheless evident that, in this respect, his work inherits the centuries-long tradition of charging each of the rival queens with different, often contrasting features: Elizabeth, with her scheming and ambition, is an entirely earthly creature, while Mary, with her dignity and moral strength, is an almost metaphysical being. Rather than the triumph of Catholic orthodoxy, her death represents the queen's elevation above the mortal struggles of her antagonist: if the red dress in which the historical figure decided to die lent itself to an unmistakable self-portrayal as a martyr, the white one that Schiller chooses for his character is a sign of her ultimately unchallenged purity.

Originally composed for Naples' Teatro San Carlo between July and August 1834, Donizetti's *Maria Stuarda* finally premiered at the Teatro alla Scala, in Milan, on 30 December 1835.[90] Based on an Italian

88 See, in particular, Kari Lokke, "Schiller's *Maria Stuart*: The Historical Sublime and the Aesthetics of Gender," *Monatshefte* 82, no. 2 (1990): 123–41, and Todd Kontje, "Staging the Sublime: Schiller's *Maria Stuart* as Ironic Tragedy," *Modern Language Studies* 22, no. 2 (1992): 88–101.

89 Schiller devoted the following works, among others, to the sublime: *On the Sublime: Toward the Further Development of Some Kantian Themes* (1793) and *On the Sublime* (1801).

90 *Maria Stuarda* was not Donizetti's only foray into Tudor-era subjects: the other three operas he composed were *Il castello di Kenilworth* (1829), *Anna Bolena* (1830), and *Roberto Devereux* (1837).

translation of Schiller's *Maria Stuart*,[91] the libretto was written by the young, inexperienced Giuseppe Bardari, who was only seventeen when Donizetti hired him. As William Ashbrook argues, the notable imbalance in age, reputation, and experience between composer and librettist might have meant that Donizetti was very much a dominant force in the genesis and writing of this libretto.[92] Bardari was far from being the composer's first choice: Felice Romani, a widely experienced librettist who had been Donizetti's close collaborator, was unavailable, so after a time-consuming search, Bardari was chosen. Donizetti had seen the Italian version of Schiller's tragedy in Milan and had decided he would compose an opera on that subject.[93] The libretto immediately drew the negative attention of Neapolitan censors, who were not fond of the regicide theme, and Bardari was forced to rewrite parts of it.[94] On top of this, the two sopranos who had been cast as Mary and Elizabeth (Giuseppina Ronzi and Anna del Sere, respectively) had massive rows during rehearsals, which disrupted the overall production.[95] Ultimately, King Ferdinand II did not allow the opera to be performed,[96] and it was only at the end of the following year that *Maria Stuarda* saw its debut at La Scala, with the legendary Maria Malibran in the title role. The story presented simplifies Schiller's original source, with some divergences: Mortimer is not present in the opera, Elizabeth's hatred for Mary is more pointed in its association with her jealousy towards Leicester, and the tone of their confrontation scene is even harsher than in the German play. Specifically, to mark its culmination, Mary calls her English enemy the "impure daughter of Boleyn" ("figlia impura di Bolena"), an "indecent, obscene whore" ("meretrice indegna e oscena"), and ultimately an "abject bastard" ("vil bastarda"), whose very reign profanes the sacredness of the English throne. As in Schiller, the opera relies heavily on the visual – and auditory – juxtaposition between the two queens, playing on their renowned rivalry to generate contempt for the one (Elizabeth)

91 The translation was authored by Andrea Maffei and published in 1830. See William Ashbrook, *Donizetti and His Operas* (Cambridge: Cambridge University Press, 1982), 84.

92 See Ashbrook, *Donizetti*, 584.

93 See Ashbrook, *Donizetti*, 84.

94 On this subject, see Jeremy Commons, "*Maria Stuarda* and the Neapolitan Censorship," *Donizetti Society Journal* 3 (1977): 151–67.

95 In one such instance Donizetti, as he famously reported, told Ronzi that "those two queens were whores, and you too are whores" (Ashbrook, *Donizetti*, 85).

96 Regarding the trials, tribulations, and radical rewritings of the libretto, see Ashbrook, *Donizetti*, 85–8.

and admiration for the other (Mary). Donizetti was the most prominent composer to deal with the story of Mary Queen of Scots, but he was not the first one to do so. The earliest was Pietro Casella with his *Maria Stuarda, Regina di Scozia*, on a libretto by Francesco Gonella (also based on Schiller), which premiered at the Teatro della Pergola in Florence in 1813. Another noteworthy *Maria Stuarda, Regina di Scozia* was composed by the then famous Saverio Mercadante and premiered at the Teatro Comunale in Bologna in 1821. The libretto for this opera was written by the prolific librettist Gaetano Rossi, who, instead of focusing on the queen's death, explored her relationship with Darnley. However, unlike Alfieri – whose tragedy he must have known – Rossi presents a wildly imaginative happy ending in which Mary, thanks to her husband, survives a plot devised by her Scottish enemies. The tragic events of 1566 are also dramatized in the two-act opera *David Riccio*, composed by Vincenzo Capecelatro on a libretto by Andrea Maffei, which premiered at La Scala in 1850, and in the three-act *David Rizzio*, with a score by Luigi Canepa and a libretto by Enrico Costa, which was staged at Milan's Teatro Carcano in 1872. Operas about the queen's life were produced until the end of the century, and in addition to them, there is also a six-act tragic ballet choreographed by Giovanni Galzerani. It was staged at La Scala in 1826: the source in this case was also Schiller. Galzerani was no stranger to Tudor subjects, having already staged (1823–4) the ballet *Elisabetta d'Inghilterra al castello di Kenilworth*, choreographed by his mentor Gaetano Gioia, which is yet another testament to Italian interest in the fictionalized remnants of English affairs.

Although operas continued to be composed during the twentieth century,[97] the advent of cinema and, subsequently, television, opened new avenues in the fictional reworkings of the myth. Already in 1895, *The Execution of Mary, Queen of Scots*, produced by Alfred Clark, marked the queen's entrance in the seventh art as well as the first ever instance of film editing, which made it possible to screen a realistic beheading. John Ford, who would make a name for himself as a director of classic Westerns such as *Stagecoach* (1939), directed *Mary of Scotland* (1936), featuring Katharine Hepburn in the title role. British stars Vanessa Redgrave and Glenda Jackson were Mary and Elizabeth in *Mary Queen of Scots* (1971), directed by Charles Jarrott, and most recently, the roles

97 Perhaps the most successful among them is *Mary, Queen of Scots* (1977), composed by Thea Musgrave, who also wrote the libretto (adapted from Peruvian-born author Amalia Elguera's play *Moray*). The opera focuses on the years between Mary's return to Scotland and her arrival in England.

were taken on by, respectively, Saoirse Ronan and Margot Robbie in the 2018 movie directed by Josie Rourke and inspired by John Guy's biography *My Heart Is My Own*. Alongside these and other cinematic productions, the early life of the Scottish queen was a source for the TV series *Reign*, created by Stephanie SenGupta and Laurie McCarthy, which ran for four seasons from 2013 to 2017. A teen drama set in an early modern France rife with anachronisms, faux pas, and *Gossip Girl*–style storylines, *Reign* has attracted abundant criticism for its patent oversimplification of historical materials, to the point that *USA Today*'s Robert Bianco unceremoniously opened his review by asking whether it would be too much for the network "to avoid making [young viewers] stupid"[98] if educating them was not their goal. However problematic, this latter development – or, more properly, twisting – of the story of Mary Queen of Scots bears witness to the endless fascination that it bears on the collective imagination.

From Della Valle's solemn martyr of Catholicism to a love rival and a political enemy, and to a sweet but feisty young princess who just wants to have fun with her girlfriends, Mary's foreboding wish that her story be remembered and celebrated long after its end appears to have been granted. The early portrayal of the Queen of Scots provided in the tragedy that is presented here bears witness to the beginning of a literary canonization whose fundamental elements – resistance, power, ultimate sacrifice – became enduring themes across time, ideologies, and genres.

98 Robert Bianco, "Wrong as *Reign*: CW ignores history, insults viewers," *USA Today* (16 October 2013), https://www.usatoday.com/story/life/tv/2013/10/16/reign-review/2994343/ (accessed 7 February 2021). More broadly, on the fortune of this subject matter in film, see Susan Doran and Thomas Freeman, eds., *Tudors and Stuarts on Film: Historical Perspectives* (London: Macmillan Education, 2008).

Chronology of Mary Queen of Scots and Her Times[1]

1533 (January)	Henry VIII marries Anne Boleyn
1533 (September)	Elizabeth is born
1534 (November)	First Act of Supremacy
1536 (May)	Anne Boleyn is executed
1542 (December)	Mary is born
1543 (September)	Mary is crowned Queen of Scots
1547 (January)	Henry VIII dies
1548 (July)	Mary is off to France
1558 (April)	Mary marries the dauphin Francis
1558 (November)	Elizabeth is crowned Queen of England
1559 (July)	Mary becomes queen consort of France
1560 (December)	Francis II dies
1561 (August)	Mary is back in Scotland
1564 (March)	Elizabeth pressures Mary to marry Robert Dudley, Earl of Leicester
1565 (July)	Mary marries Henry Stuart, Lord Darnley
1566 (March)	Davide Rizzio is assassinated
1566 (June)	James is born
1567 (February)	Darnley is assassinated
1567 (May)	Mary marries James Hepburn, Lord Bothwell

1 For a more detailed chronology of Mary Queen of Scots, see Guy, *My Heart*, 516–20.

1567 (June)	Mary is imprisoned at Lochleven
1567 (July)	Mary is forced to abdicate and James VI is crowned King of Scots
1568 (May)	Mary escapes and seeks refuge in England
1568 (October–December)	Mary is imprisoned and trial for the death of Darnley begins
1569 (January)	Mary is found neither guilty nor innocent
1571 (November)	George Buchanan publishes the *Detectioun*
1583 (November)	Throckmorton Plot is discovered
1586 (August)	Babington Plot is discovered
1586 (September–October)	Mary arrives at Fotheringhay and trial begins
1586 (October)	Mary is found guilty
1587 (February)	Elizabeth signs Mary's death warrant
1587 (February)	Mary is executed
1588 (August)	The Spanish Armada is defeated by Elizabeth's fleet
1603 (March)	Elizabeth dies
1603 (July)	James VI is crowned King of England, Scotland, and Ireland as James I

Note on Translation and Commentary

Translating early modern verse is never an easy feat, and translating Federico Della Valle's *La reina di Scotia* is no exception. When rendering it into English, my goal has been to preserve the linguistic peculiarities of the text as much as possible and, at the same time, make it accessible for a contemporary English-speaking reader. The process has involved many decisions, the first of which had to do with the title itself of the tragedy. Instead of going for a literal rendering – *The Queen of Scotland* – I have opted to use Mary's actual title – *The Queen of Scots* – which reflects the Latin title *rex Scotorum* that Scottish sovereigns had used since the Middle Ages. Besides being more historically accurate, this is how she is known still today in the anglophone world, so this seemed to be the best way to go about presenting this tragedy in English for the first time. In the same way as I opted for a target culture–appropriate rendering of the title, I have anglicized all character names. In the context of early modern Italian works about an Anglo-Scottish historical subject, this has entailed a process of de-Italianization of all identifiable English-related names (of people and places), unless otherwise noted. For instance, the "Conte di Pembrocia" has been rendered as the "Earl of Pembroke," but the "Conte di Mestrice," in Sartorio Loschi's *Letter Concerning the Death of the Queen of Scots* (in the Appendix), has been rendered as the "Earl of Mestrice" because it is unclear which English name was being referenced. Della Valle's poetic language is one of great complexity, often deliberately difficult in its syntactical organization – not least because of metric constraints – more so than in its lexical construction. The *endecasillabi* and *settonari* that make up the tragedy have been rendered in free verse, in which I have tried to respect the original structure as much as possible, reserving the most radical divergences to the cases in which English fluency would have been severely compromised. The general principle that I have followed, therefore, was to

strike a balance between maintaining some of the challenges that the text presents for a contemporary Italian reader, while not entirely abdicating the translator's role as, first and foremost, a go-between. In the same way, my footnotes mostly refer to the English translation, but with attention to the Italian original, especially where noteworthy rhetorical figures are used which might be otherwise lost, or less effective, in the target language. The elements highlighted in the annotations cover a variety of issues, from historical context, scholarly sources, and literary references to poetic devices and dramaturgical clarifications. My intent is to provide something resembling a running commentary to benefit the broadest possible range of readers, angles, and interests.

My translation was conducted using the 1628 *editio princeps*, with the parallel consultation of modern critical editions by Roberto Cazzani (Milan: Mondadori, 1955), Andrea Gareffi (Milan: Mursia, 1988), Maria Gabriella Stassi (Turin: UTET, 1995), and Matteo Durante (Messina: Sicania, 2005).

The Queen of Scots

TO THE SUPREME PONTIFF AND OUR LORD
URBAN VIII

Most Blessed Father

In your youthful years, Your Holiness honoured the bones of Mary Queen of Scots with a most ingenious epitaph written by the most eloquent Scotsman Conn, which will forever be admired in the life of the queen.[1] This was a work of utmost piety, suited to the noblest and holiest of natures. And since in it you showed an affectionate inclination towards the merits of that Queen, I can presume that hearing of her memory shall not be an unwelcome interruption of Your Holiness' noble occupations. With this in mind and with all due reverence, the tragically described progress of that strange death dares to present itself before your Sacred person; and in presenting it, Holy Father, I humbly bow before your most Blessed feet.

La reina di Scotia

AL SOMMO PONTEFICE ET SIGNOR NOSTRO
URBANO VIII

Beatissimo Padre

Piacque ai giovenili anni di Vostra Santità d'onorar l'ossa di Maria Reina di Scozia, con l'ingegnosissimo epitafio, che potrà ammirarsi perpetuo nella vita di lei, scritta dall' eloquentissimo Coneo scoto. Fu l'opra di chiara pietà, né men propria a nobilissima e spiritosa natura. E come in lei si vide affettuosa inclinazione ai meriti di quella Reina, così può stimarsi che l'udir sue memorie non debba essere discara intermission all'altissime occupazioni di Vostra Santità. Con opinion tale, ma colmi anche di devutissima sommessione, osano di presentarsi al suo Sacrato aspetto i progressi di quella strana morte, tragicamente descritti; e, presentandogli, umilissimo adora, Santissimo Padre, I vostri Beatissimi piedi

1 The epitaph, *De nece reginae Scotiae*, was written in the immediate aftermath of the queen's execution. As he declares in the dedication, Della Valle read it when it was printed as a paratext in George Conn's *Vita Mariae Stuartae Scotiae Reginae*. A few years later, the epitaph was included in the pope's collection of poems, *Poemata* (Rome: Collegium Romanum Societatis Jesu, 1631). On this, see Introduction, p. 14, and Villani, "From Mary."

Dramatis Personae

SHADE OF THE KING OF FRANCE
QUEEN OF SCOTS
LADY-IN-WAITING
CHORUS OF DAMSELS
SERVANT
COUNSELLOR OF THE QUEEN OF ENGLAND
EARL OF PEMBROKE
EARL OF CUMBERLAND
BUTLER OF THE QUEEN OF SCOTS
ARCHER
MESSENGER
MACE BEARER
EXECUTIONER

Persone che parlano

OMBRA DEL RE DI FRANCIA
REINA DI SCOZIA
CAMERIERA
CORO DI DAMIGELLE
SERVO
CONSIGLIERO DELLA REINA D'INGHILTERR.
CONTE DI PEMBROCIA
CONTE DI COMBERLANDIA
MAGGIORDUOMO DELLA REINA DI SCOZIA
ARCIERO
MESSO
MAZZIERO
CARNEFICE

SHADE OF THE KING OF FRANCE:[2]

A mountain rises in the air, held up by clouds,
and spirits roam around its wretched foot:[3]
slow and foolish spirits
who wandered among you, falling leaves,
and kept sinning from day to year,

OMBRA DEL RE DI FRANCIA:

Monte è ne l'aria, e il sostengon nembi,
al cui penoso piè s'aggiran spirti;
spirti, che stolti e lenti
errando già fra voi, foglie cadenti,
trassero i falli lor dal giorno a l'anno,

2 The Shade of the King of France serves as a prologue to the dramatic action; it was added to the 1628 printed edition.

3 The reference is to Purgatory, and specifically to its image as a mountain – as opposed to the pit of Hell – created by Dante in the *Divine Comedy*. The spirits mentioned are the souls of the people who are slowly and painfully climbing it in order to finally atone their sins and be admitted to Heaven (see "[…] quel secondo regno / dove l'umano spirito si purga / e di salire al ciel diventa degno," *Purgatory* I, 4–7). On the function and re-elaboration of this image here, see Federico Della Valle, *Tutte le opere*, ed. Pietro Cazzani (Milan: Mondadori, 1955), 478; see also Sanguineti White, *Dal detto alla figura*, 49–50.

with little care;
until they ended sins and life
with a sigh
of rightful sense.[4]
They now regret their faults and lateness
with desperate sorrow, yet they keep hoping.
To such people and unknown region
belongs this shade or spirit or ghost,
which you now hear and barely see.
Still, whatever I be called, I was
once one of you,
but elevated
by a royal crown and mantle:[5]
oh, so heavy to bear![6]
I was revered by the Seine and the Garonne
and the long coast towards the sky of the Ursae,
and its opposite, where salty dead waters
turn the Rhône into sea.[7]
But for what? Reverence and sceptres
surrendered to a bit of dark soil,
to burial:

senza sentirne affanno;
alfin con un sospiro
di consigliato senno
falli e vita finiro:
or piangono l'error e la tardanza
in disperato duol, ma con speranza.
Di gente tal, di region sì ignota
è questa, ch'or udite e mal vedete,
ombra o spirto o fantasma.
Pur, qualunque io sia detto, certo fui
alcun tempo un di voi,
senonché mi distinse
regia corona e manto,
gravi a portarsi, ahi quanto!
A me tributo diêr Senna e Garonna
e lungo lido verso il ciel de l'Orse,
con altro opposto, ov'acque morte amare
il Rodano fan mare.
Ma che giovò? Cesser tributi e scettri
a poca terra oscura,
chiamata sepoltura:

---

4 In Dantean fashion, the souls repented their sins before they died, which is a necessary condition to access Purgatory. The opening of *The Queen of Scots*, therefore, presents the central doctrinal theme of the tragedy right from the start: the acknowledgment of one's sins, leading to salvation, as opposed to proud sinfulness, resulting in eternal damnation.

5 The Shade speaking is that of Francis II (1544–1560), king of France (r. 1559–1560), first husband of Mary Queen of Scots and king consort of Scotland (1558–1560). Francis was the eldest son of Henry II and Catherine de' Medici.

6 Royalty is both an honour and a burden.

7 The Seine, the Garonne, and the Rhône are French rivers.

a horrible place, which finds dignity	orrida stanza, pur tanto ha di degno,
in calmly hosting	che 'n lei riposan cheti
beggars and kings, sharp opposites,	mendicitate e regno, aspri contrari
in deathly rest.	ai riposi mortali.
I left there what was visible;	In lei lasciai di me quel che si vide;
the invisible I carry with me	l'invisibil portai e meco stassi,
not as clear as it once was,	chiaro no, qual pria l'ebbi,
but stained by earthly s orrows,	ma tinto in ombra di terrene cure,
now turned into bitter tears.	fatte or lagrime dure.
I loved a woman queen, and my love	Amai donna reina, e fu l'amarla
was fair, for she was my wife and bones.	giusto, perché fu moglie e ossa mie:
But the pain of leaving her	ma 'l dolor di lasciarla,
was unbearable; and my guilt is, too.	come soverchio fu, così fu colpa.
Now, of this and other faults	Di questa e d'altre or sento
more painful is the wound,	più viva la ferita,
just as after earthly death,	quanto, morto il mortale,
life is more alive to me.	ha più viva la vita.
Thus I wander and suffer	Tal erro e tal mi doglio, e talor miro
and observe the whirling wheel	dei mondani successi
of human fortune:[8]	il variabil giro.
alas, it would be better not to,	Lasso, e il non veder fôra assai meglio,
for in it do I see	poscia che miro in loro
the worst of every misfortune!	d'ogni sciagura il peggio!
I see the flesh and bones	Veggio la carne e l'ossa,
that in dying I left alive among you,	che morendo io lasciai vive fra voi,
that I left on a throne with sublime crowns:	lasciai regnanti con corone eccelse,

8 The reference here is to the ancient symbol of the wheel of fortune (in Latin, *fortunae rota*), characterizing the fickleness and unpredictability of earthly existence.

she is a prisoner, a servant, and – yet more
terrible and tearful –
I see[9] her go towards the fatal blow
of an infamous, wounding blade fit only
for the blood of ill-born sinners.[10]
In such excesses, who would think it strange
that the voice of a pious lover
make itself heard lamenting the offence?
May my dead body rise from the grave
to avenge it!
But here comes the unfortunate woman:
how she has changed
from how I left her,
from what I hoped for her!
Oh, my flesh, you were adorned
with royal pomp and a golden mantle:
now you're clad in pitiful
beggar's robes!
Born to reign, so you reigned:
now, like a servant, doomed
by twenty years of miserable martyrdom,
you will be brought to death.
Oh, who can know God's plan,
or understand its ends?
Revere and tremble, most wretched children
of errant Eve!

or prigioniere, or serve, e, quel ch'è 'l sommo
di lagrime e sventura,
condursi al colpo estremo
di ferro feritor infame, avezzo
al sangue solo di malnati rei.
In tanto eccesso, a chi parer dee strano
che voce di pio amante
si faccia udir a lamentarne il danno?
Sorga pur di tomba anco il braccio morto
a vendicarne il torto!
Ma di là appar la sventurata donna,
ahi, ahi dissimil quanto
a quel ch'io la lasciai,
a quel ch'io la sperai!
Rimanesti, o mia carne,
di regia pompa e d'aureo manto adorna:
or ti cinge, mendica,
miserabil gonna!
Rimanesti a regnar, a regnar nata:
or, qual serva, dannata
da vent'anni di misero martìre,
verrai tratta a morire!
Deh, chi giunge a veder gli alti consigli,
o chi scerner può 'l fine?
Adorate e tremate, o d'Eva errante
miserissimi figli!

9 The verbs connected to the semantic sphere of sight are prominent in these lines.

10 The Shade makes it clear early on that Mary's death cannot be avoided: what the tragedy will portray is her progress towards it, and her acceptance of her divinely ordained fate.

QUEEN:
If anyone, in the whirling wheel
of mortal life,[11]
seeks to know how one can fall
from the happy heights of fortune
to an abyss of pain,
to the unhappiest, lowest state,
hear my thoughts and behold me.
Behold me,[12] who was once a queen
with two illustrious crowns and sceptres,
which at once ruled over French and Scots:[13]
daughter of a king, wife of a mighty king,
descended from a long line of kings,
and mother to a king.[14]
Now I am trapped within these walls,
a prisoner tied to another's might and whims,

REINA:
Se pur è alcun, che nel volubil giro
de le cose mortali
cerchi come si caggia o si ruine
da nubi di fortuna alte e felici
a dolorosi abissi
di sorti infelicissime, meschine,
senta me che ragiono, e me rimiri.
Rimiri me, che già reina adorna
di due chiare corone e di due scettri,
che resser ad un tempo Franchi e Scoti,
figlia di re, moglie di re possente,
discesa per lungo ordine da regi,
e di re madre ancora,
or chiusa in mura anguste, or prigioniera,
legata a l'altrui forza, a l'altrui voglia,

11 Another reference to the wheel of fortune. The Queen's first monologue presents a pounding sequence of antitheses, opposing images and concepts joined together in speech. On the use of antithesis in these lines, see Durante, "La Maria Stuarda dellavalliana," 351–2.

12 *Coblas capfinidas*, that is, the repetition of the end of the previous verse at the beginning of the new one ("[…] behold me. / Behold me […]"; "[…] me rimiri. / Rimiri me […]"). In Italian, the repetition is also a chiasmus, which cannot be rendered into English.

13 Having become queen of Scotland upon the death of her father, James V, when she was five days old (14 December 1542), Mary reigned until 1567, when she was forced to abdicate. As the wife of Francis II, she also held the title of queen consort of France until her husband's death. See Introduction, p. 5, and Chronology.

14 The first of several self-portraits. Mary defines herself – and her royal stature – by referencing her functions in relation to the men of life, which she uses to reclaim her exceptionality. The husband that she references is Francis II, who was the first of three men she married. The son is James VI. Mary's only child, he was born out of her second marriage, with Henry Stuart, Lord Darnley. James became king of Scotland following his mother's forced abdication in 1567 at merely one year of age, and succeeded his mother's rival, Elizabeth I, to the throne of England and Ireland in 1603.

deprived, if not of majesty
or royal power – of which my name
painfully reminds me –
wretched, but deprived also
of what nature gives freely, of the calm air
which nourishes things alive:
I spend my nights and days among the risks and pains
of death and life.
But if it is true that obscure laws
and various ways –
now painful, now happy –
govern man's condition,
oh, powerful invisible hand,[15]
how can it be that after the span
of twenty unhappy years,[16] my misery or life
has not come to an end
or at least been altered? And yet I cannot,
if I look back at the ills and misfortunes
which are well used to tormenting
us poor mortals,
I cannot think what I have not experienced
in all of my sorrows
and of my offences.
Captive queen,
disconsolate widow, abandoned

priva, non dirò già di maestade
o d'impero real, ché di ciò 'l nome
a pena mi rimembra,
misera, ma priva anco
di quel che dà natura aere sereno
a nodrir quanto ha vita,
passo le notti e i dì fra i rischi e i danni
e di morte e di vita.
Ma s'è pur ver che con incerta norma
e con vario costume,
or doloroso, or lieto,
volve lo stato umano
possente ascosa mano,
com'esser può che dopo 'l lungo corso
di vent'anni infelici al fin non giunga,
o non si muti almeno,
la miseria o la vita? E pur non posso,
se ben rincorro le sciagure e i mali,
a tormentar avezzi
miseri mortali,
non posso ritrovar quel che più manchi
al colmo del mio affanno,
al sommo del mio danno:
reina prigioniera,
vedova sconsolata, abbandonata

15 The invisible hand is an image of the Divine Providence. References to its inscrutability abound throughout the tragedy.

16 In actuality, Mary's detention lasted a little under nineteen years, from May 1568 until her death on 8 February 1587. Della Valle is not the only one to identify the duration as twenty years (a more convenient round number), which is in fact almost universally shared by commentators and authors of fiction. The long detention is exploited in this tragedy as a kind of purgatorial path, leading her to the final acceptance of her end (see also Durante, "La Maria Stuarda dellavalliana," 365).

mother of a useless son,
mistress of a rebellious, treacherous people,[17]
woman without counsel,
destitute, ill, of decaying age.
Is this all I can say, or can life
devise more sorrows?
Alas, is there no other place
where sorrows can be, but in my own self?
I alone with all torments;
nothing, nothing to comfort me!
How darkly and cruelly
did you move, oh sun, on that day when the impious shores,
the impious shores and deceitful, heinous sands
of England did my unhappy feet touch,
which brought me there as a queen
with crown and honours,
but with the fate of a servant,
abducted and chained![18]
Alas! Yet I was born,
I was born the daughter of a king, and the heiress
of an ancient kingdom;
I was the wife of a glorious king, and the mother
of a king, who from me inherits
mantle and sceptre and crown;
to such heights did Heaven lift me,
so that I, in falling, might plummet
to not being mistress

madre d'inutil figlio,
signora di rubella infida gente,
donna senza consiglio,
povera, inferma ed in età cadente.
Poss'io più dir, o può formar la vita
altre nuove sciagure?
O non ha luogo, lassa,
ove le impieghi, se non in me sola?
Sola, e tutto al tormento;
Nulla, ahi nulla al contento!
Deh, come oscuro e crudo
rotasti, o sol, quel dì che l'empio lido,
empio lido e spergiura infame arena
d'Inghilterra, toccò l'infausto piede,
che me portò con nome di reina
coronata, onorata,
e con destin di serva
rapita, catenata!
Lassa me! Dunque nacqui,
nacqui figlia di re, fui poscia erede
d'antichissimo regno,
d'eccelso re fui moglie, e son madre anco
di re, che da me prende
manto e scettro e corona:
a tanto colmo alzar mi volse il Cielo,
perch'io cadendo poi precipitassi
a non esser più donna

17 The second of her self-portraits, this time entirely in the negative: a queen that is also a prisoner, a wife who has lost her husband, a mother who cannot rely on her son's help, a sovereign betrayed by her subjects. For more on this technique, see Introduction, pp. 25–6.

18 She references her fatal arrival in England, lured by Elizabeth's promise of asylum (May 1568). See Introduction, p. 6, and Chronology.

even of myself;[19]	neanco di me stessa,
and that from a tyrannical hand	e da mano tiranna
I may keep this life	ritener questa vita,
almost as a favour and mercy	quasi grazia e mercede
from my impious enemy.[20]	d'un'empia mia nemica.
Oh evil fate, oh misfortune,	Ahi ria sorte, ahi sventura,
oh sorrow, oh pain,	ahi affanno, ahi dolore,
how is my heart not to break?[21]	come non spezzi il core?
LADY-IN-WAITING:[22] What dire memories	CAMERIERA: Deh, quai memorie dure
you bring back to memory,	a la memoria torni,
to double the pain!	per raddoppiare il male!
Which, though it afflicts and torments us,	Il qual, se ben ci affligge e ci tormenta,
seems to be felt less	par che col non parlarne
with not being spoken.	assai meno si senta.
Still, since lament goes with pain,	Pur, poscia che col duol sen va il lamento,
as wind with clouds,	come con nube vento,
let there be no one to blame,	alcun non sia ch'accusi,
my mistress and queen, your complaints;	donna e reina mia, le tue querele;

19 She recognizes – but, as will be shown, still has not come to terms with – the fact that Divine Providence has selected her as an example: her path through misery towards death is part of God's inscrutable plan.

20 The material agent in her misfortunes is Elizabeth, whom she immediately qualifies as impious. In Mary's view, she is doubly so: first, because she is a Protestant, and second, because she has dared defile the sacred body of an anointed queen such as herself. This is one of many occurrences of the theme of the sacredness of sovereigns. Although she does not name her enemy, she nonetheless qualifies her in the feminine ("nemica").

21 Erasmo G. Gerato remarks that these final verses echo Count Ugolino's in *Inferno* XXXIII ("ahi dura terra, perché non t'apristi"). See "Un'anima traviata: *La Reina di Scotia* di Federico Della Valle," *Neuphilologische Mitteilungen* 81, no. 1 (1980): 7–14, 12.

22 The Lady-in-Waiting is possibly modelled on the figure of Jane Kennedy (d. 1589), who had been Mary's companion since before her imprisonment. Della Valle's characterization of her, however, is more symbolic than historical: she represents the old guard, a vestige of Mary's past grandeur. A faithful source of support during her last moments on earth, she simultaneously serves as a mother, sister, and daughter figure. In the seventeenth-century Italian dramatic canon, Jane Kennedy is present as the character "Queneda" in Domenico Gisberti's three-act tragedy *La barbarie del caso* (1664).

nor does this servant of yours intend	né questa serva tua tanto presume
or dare to do. To me it befalls to suffer	o tanto ardisce. A me dolermi tocca
your pain, and to tune	col tuo dolor e accordar al suono
my sighs to your sighs and tears.[23]	dei tuoi sospiri i miei sospiri e 'l pianto;
But, if royal goodness and ancient fidelity	ma se talor concede
may once allow	bontà reale e fedeltade antica
affection to say what it feels,	dir quel che sente affezionata voglia,
to lessen your sorrow and my worry,	per scemar in te 'l duolo e in me l'affanno,
I shall remember among the memories of youth	rimembrerò fra le memorie acerbe
your sweet hopes and the secrets	le tue dolci speranze e quei secreti,
that you only shared with me and that I hide,	ch'a me sola confidi e ch'io nascondo,
if possible, to my very own self,	se far si puote, al mio medesmo seno,
to give them back to you. Thinking of which,	per tornargli a te sola. A' quai pensando,
what must I say, my dearly beloved queen?	che debb'io dir, reina amata e cara?
Are there new reasons for new laments	Sorgon nuove cagioni a nuovi lai,
which you hide and don't speak? Or are you suffering	e tu le ascondi e taci? O pur ti duoli
for your old, persistent pains and thus give voice	di lunga antica doglia, e dài principio
to the gravest laments, when evil	a più gravi lamenti, allorché 'l male
is coming to an end? For evil is coming	è per giungere al fin? Ché ben al fine
to an end,	è per giungere il male,
if what you told me is true, or if it's true	se 'l vero a me dicesti, o se 'l ver dice

23 These lines emphasize the close relationship between Mary and the Lady-in-Waiting. Throughout the tragedy, this female bond – which at times, especially towards the end, takes the shape of a mother-daughter tie – serves as counterpoint to the female rivalry between the two queens, which ultimately represents its perversion.

what the king, your dear son, writes;
he promises to wage war
upon the English kingdom,
with Scottish and Spanish forces joined;
and he also promises
to shed his own blood and give his life
as sacrifice and price
for your freedom,[24] if the cruel woman
who keeps you here
will not give you back to your kingdom and your Scots,
released and free as part of a deal or peace,
which is likely being debated or signed.[25]
Thus must we hope. Nor is it worth
believing that a cruel tyrant, not loved
by her people which is divided into factions and sects,
a weak woman[26]
who is used to devising traps in times of peace
would willingly take on a war
against two powerful, united kingdoms

quei che ne scrive il re, caro tuo figlio.
Il qual promette certa
la guerra al regno inglese, aggiunte insieme
l'armi scote a l'ispane;
e più anco promette:
il suo sangue e la vita
per sacrificio e prezzo
de la tua libertà, quando la cruda,
che qui ti tien rinchiusa,
non ti renda al tuo regno e ai tuoi Scoti
libera e sciolta per accordo o pace;
la qual forse or si tratta o è conchiusa.
Così sperar debbiam! Né già conviene
stimar ch'aspra tiranna, e poco cara
al popol suo, diviso in parti e 'n sètte,
e che femina imbelle,
sol fra la pace avezza a tesser frodi,
volontaria riceva anzi la guerra
di due regni possenti insieme uniti,

24 The theme of James' alleged preparations for his mother's freedom is repeated throughout the dramatic action. Bearing little historical accuracy, its function is mainly to keep Mary's and her supporters' hopes alive, as well as to enhance the image of a tight motherly bond between her and her son. Della Valle uses his figure, as the only survivor of Mary's men, to substantiate the implicit claim that the queen had neither been forgotten (the servants attest to this) nor abandoned.

25 Again, nothing will come out of these conjectures.

26 Yet another ungenerous portrait of Elizabeth, specifically relying on the oxymoronic claim that she is both a tyrant and a weak woman. It is noteworthy that the Lady-in-Waiting carefully avoids bestowing the title of queen upon her.

which can assault her from land and sea,
rather than freeing the woman whom she keeps entrapped
beyond all rights and against customs
of humanity and faith, against all laws
both barbaric and civil. Or, if her cruel hand
shuts her ears and takes away her senses
of judgment and prudence, making her wait
obstinately for war, this may be a plan
of the Divine Providence[27] to punish her
for her many faults, her many deceits,
her cruelty, her wrongs, her rebellious
and false opinions, her false worship
of the impious religion which is an enemy to heaven.[28]
And from this I see the promise
of certain freedom, which you well deserve
after so long and hard a captivity.[29]
Times change, and in changing, they bring

che da terra e da mar ponno assalirla,
che liberar colei, ch'ella ritiene
oltra ogni dritto, contra ogni costume
d'umanità, di fé, contra ogni legge
o barbara o gentil. O, se pur chiude
man dura a lei gli orecchi e toglie i sensi
di senno e avvedimento, ond'ostinata
la guerra aspetti, quinci forse ordisce
Providenza divina a lei la pena
dovuta a tante colpe, a tanti inganni,
a la perfidia, ai torti, a la rubella
e falsa opinion, al falso culto
d'empia religion nemica al Cielo.
E quinci libertà veggio promessa
sicura e certa a te, che ben la merti,
dopo sì lunga prigionia e sì dura.
Giransi i tempi, e raggirando seco

27 An explicit mention of the inscrutable hands that move human existence.

28 The tirade against Protestantism has materialized: the battle between Mary and Elizabeth is parallel to the battle between the Church of Rome and the Church of England.

29 The promise of freedom – substantiated by the expectation of James' war on England as part of God's plan – plays a major role in the Lady-in-Waiting's rhetoric: besides serving as a source of reassurance for Mary, her insistence betrays her own need to deny what is inevitably going to unfold.

about new fates: what seems	s'aggiran nuove sorti, e quel che sembra
impossible one day happens in the next.	impossibil un dì, ne l'altro fassi.
Constant begging and humble suffering	Continui preghi e umil sofferenza
are painful to the heavens.	al Ciel fan violenza:
This reveals and promises	così dice e promette
a holy faithful voice; and you who have been	santa voce fedel; e tu molt'anni
suffering, bent, and demure for long years,	sofferente, pieghevole e dimessa
withstand this fatal weight and pray.	sotto 'l peso fatal sostieni e preghi.
If the earth lack arms, and if human minds	Manchin l'armi a la terra, e manchi 'l dritto
lack rightfulness and pity:	e la pietà qui fra le menti umane:
will celestial intelligence	mancherà forse a le celesti menti
not fulfil its promises?	la fede a le promesse?
Furthermore, your cruel enemy	Segue a questo che l'aspra tua nemica
offers conditions for your liberation	offre condizioni, onde tu possa
if you wish to accept them, but if they are too harsh	liberarti, se vuoi; che se son dure
and you refuse them, let them at least	e le ricusi tu, vagliano almeno
be a symbol of good hope among so many evils.[30]	per speranza di ben fra tanti mali:
Those who can have some hope of deliverance	di nulla si disperi,
must not despair.	chi aver può cosa, in cui refugio speri.
Besides, she confirms you will keep your life	Oltreché, t'assicura ella la vita
through her letters, as you saw	con le lettere sue, come vedesti
but few days ago, and she promises she will not consent	pochi dì son, né consentir promette

30 This is a foreshadowing of the inflammatory, outrageously unacceptable conditions proposed by Elizabeth through her emissaries later on. See vv. 874–903.

that your royal person be offended	che la real persona tua s'offenda
beyond imprisonment, which is unjust,	fuorché di prigionia. La qual è ingiusta,
and undeniably harsh and perilous.	né già si può negar, è acerba e grave:
But what, then? Is there no room left	ma che? Luogo non resta
for violence or deceit? Let there be room then	né a forza, né ad inganno? Resti dunque
for suffering and hope, and if freedom is denied	a sofferenza, a speme, e se si niega
to the body, may the soul not be prevented	la libertade al corpo, non si tolga
from waiting for it.[31] What's right and true	a l'alma l'aspettarla. Il dritto e 'l vero
was never vanquished: such victory	mai non rimaser vinti, ed è vittoria
is beautiful, and it amends for past offenses	bellissima, che ben ristora i danni
with the highest glory,	con fregi alti di gloria,
the one which stems	quella che sorge e nasce
from the fields of sorrow.	dai campi degli affanni.
QUEEN: My victory will be in burial![32]	REINA: Mia vittoria sarà la sepoltura!
There I will raise the trophy	Ivi alzerò il trofeo
of her cruelty and of my offence	de l'altrui crudeltade e del mio danno
with a bit of dark soil.	con poca terra oscura.
And you, moved by faithful affection,	E tu, ch'or mossa da fedele affetto,
which is dear to me, though useless,	gradito e caro inver, ma inutil forse,

31 The foreshadowing continues. The ambivalence of Elizabeth's attitude is reinforced by the reference to her letters, in which she allegedly promised not to harm her prisoner and fellow queen. The final dichotomy between the deliverance of the body and that of soul will come back incessantly towards the end.

32 The theme of sacrifice is forcefully brought to the fore. In this case – and the following three lines support this idea – the struggle is entirely human, between her and her earthly enemy; its spiritual implications, specifically in the form of the clash between heresy and orthodoxy, are overshadowed by a very human game of power.

argue and talk and seek to justify	argomenti e discorri e ragion cerchi
the changing mundane things,	dal variar de le mondane cose,
another's promises, my merits,	da le promesse altrui, dai merti miei
what's right and true and never vanquished,	e dal dritto e dal ver non vinto mai,
yet maybe what you say is not what you think. Or	forse altro pensi e altro parli. O pure
have you forgotten the day, four months ago,	non ti sovien del dì, che a me veniro,
when Lord and Beale[33] came to me,	or quattro mesi son, Lord e Beelle,
those impious ministers of an impious, cruel woman,[34]	empi ministri di donna empia e cruda,
with haughty words to take away my regalia	con superbe parole a tôrmi i segni
and royal objects,	e gli arredi reali,
and, if it can even be done, the very title of queen,	e, s'esser puote, il titol di reina,
announcing my death, seated	pronunziandomi morte, a seder posti
beside me, as if I were a commoner.[35]	a lato a me, come a privata donna.
Alas, what did they say, what did I hear?	Lassa, che disser essi, e io che intesi?
Oh, their words, and their attitude,	Quai furon le parole e quali i modi,

33 Thomas Sackville, Lord Buckhurst (1536–1608) and Robert Beale (1541–1601). The presence of Buckhurst at the pronouncement of Mary's death sentence is the object of dispute: while it was generally accepted that he accompanied Beale, John Guy does not mention him in the biography *My Heart Is My Own*. The episode referenced here is not the reading of the death warrant (signed by Elizabeth), which will happen later, but rather only the communication to Mary that her trial – for the role she had allegedly played in the Babington Plot (aiming to assassinate Elizabeth) – had found her guilty and recommended her execution. See Introduction, p. 7, and Chronology.

34 Elizabeth is defined by periphrases, such as "impious, cruel woman," before she is explicitly named.

35 Mary adamantly refuses to be treated as less than an anointed sovereign, and reinforces the idea that, whatever might happen, no one could ever take her God-given title away from her.

so arrogant, dear God, and so harsh and vile!
I answered thus, and made known to them
cruel Elizabeth's[36] offence and her injustice;
but hearing me was mercy for them,
and talking to such people was pain for me,
and deadly grief,
whose remembrance kills all hope.

LADY-IN-WAITING: An unhappy, dreadful day it was;
and I rage, and suffer, and fear, and tremble,
when I think of it. Still, no harm came of it
for us;[37] rather, less harsh
has been our fortune since that day,
for they opened up a little passage from where
we can see some semblance at least
of things outside; and friendly letters
sometimes reach us, whence you receive
advice and comfort and counsel
for your decisions; and you received
the dear letter,
which gave us life:

arroganti, Dio buono, aspri e villani!
Rispos'io sì, conoscer fei l'offesa
e l'ingiustizia d'Isabella iniqua;
ma fu l'udirmi a lor grazia e mercede,
a me pena il parlar con gente tale,
ed è mortale affanno,
anzi occide ogni speme il rimembrarlo.

CAMERIERA: Infausto, acerbo dì fu veramente;
e m'adiro, e mi doglio, e temo, e tremo,
qualor vi penso. Pur, nulla è seguito
in nostro danno poi; anzi men aspra
ci s'è mostra fortuna da quel tempo,
con apricri alcun calle onde possiamo
avisar e spiar qualche ombra almeno
de le cose di fuor; e carte amiche
ci pervengon talor, onde consigli
e conforti ricevi e lume ancora
al tuo deliberar; e quinci avuta
hai la lettera cara,
che ci tornò la vita,

36 This is the first time in which the Queen of England is named ("Isabella," in the Spanish fashion), qualified by the disparaging adjective "cruel" ("iniqua").
37 The Lady-in-Waiting continues with her forcedly optimistic outlook on the events.

your son's letter, your sweet son
and dear king, who promises to take up arms
and give his life for you, as one should
for a queen and mother. Perhaps fortune
wanted to test your virtue one last time
on that day, and to deliver the final
blow of its cruelty;[38] mortal things
increasingly pile on, until they reach the top,
and then they stop and wane and fall,
and by falling and waning[39] in the end
they go back to nothing.

QUEEN: This I believe
will be my fate.[40]

la lettera del figlio, dolce figlio
e caro re, che ti promette l'arme
e la vita in tuo pro', come conviensi
verso reina e madre. Forse volse
fortuna far quel dì l'ultima prova
di tua virtute, e dar l'estremo assalto
de la sua crudeltà: così crescendo
poggia ogni mortal cosa, e giunta al colmo,
si ferma e scema e cade,
cadendo e scemando,
giunge a la fine al nulla.

REINA: Io così stimo
che fia di me!

---

38 While the theme goes back to the overarching narrative of religious sacrifice, the lexicon employed is secular: decades prior, fortune and virtue (*fortuna* and *virtù*) had been identified by Niccolò Machiavelli as opposing powers in human life, and specifically in that of a prince. In chapter 25 of *The Prince*, the Florentine secretary had argued that fortune – i.e., the inscrutable higher plan of fate, or God – was not to be regarded as unchangeable and therefore passively accepted: rather, individual virtue – i.e., human abilities and skill – could change the course of almost half of whatever may be God-given. While still resting on the theory of free will, this specific conceptual knot in *The Prince* contributed to creating the long-lasting idea of Machiavelli's atheism. What the Lady-in-Waiting is saying here arguably originates from the same grounds and is in stark contrast to the general ideological atmosphere of Della Valle's work.

39 After the listing of factual elements that bode well for the Queen – the passage, the letters, the son's promise of support – the Lady-in-Waiting closes her speech on a rhetorical consideration punctuated by a chiasmus ("they stop and wane and fall, / and by falling and waning [...]").

40 Mary never lets go of her essential orthodoxy, refusing the possibility that her fate may change: God's plan will be fulfilled regardless of any effort to alter it. Later on, we will see how Mary's position becomes slightly mitigated in this respect.

LADY-IN-WAITING: Rather than the misfortune which oppresses you now. May heavens turn your foreboding to the better, and lift the vanquished soul from pain to hope, which is sweet food to a heart starved of good and full of evil.	CAMERIERA: Anzi de la sventura, che presente ti preme. Volga il Cielo in meglio i tuoi presagi, e l'alma vinta da l'affanno sollevi a le speranze, che son soave cibo a cor, di ben digiuno e già sazio di male.
QUEEN: Misery and hope are enemies,[41] for hope is happy and cannot sprout in a field of sorrow.	REINA: Son nemiche fra loro la miseria e la speme, ch'essendo lieta, mal germoglia o nasce nel terren del dolore.
LADY-IN-WAITING: But if virtue waters it, it sprouts and grows and thrives.	CAMERIERA: Ma se virtù l'irriga, e nasce e cresce e pasce.
QUEEN: Virtue is barren if it's not moistened by heavenly dew,[42] and for me, I believe, heaven stopped its workings and stands still, perhaps looking at what a wretched, abandoned woman at last will do.	REINA: Arida vien virtù, se non ha umore da celeste rugiada, e per me il Cielo cessa or, credo, da l'opre e fermo stassi, forse a mirar quel che farà alfin donna misera abbandonata.

41 In Italian, misery and hope are feminine nouns ("miseria" and "speranza") and therefore Mary describes them as enemies in the feminine ("nemiche"): they are female enemies just like she and Elizabeth.

42 Yet again, Mary stresses her orthodoxy in subjecting her virtue to the higher workings of God. The lexical choices ("arida," "umore," "celeste rugiada") also seem to point to a sexual semantics, which would be appropriate to the context of mysticism.

LADY-IN-WAITING: Alas, what do I hear!
What are you saying, my queen! Please,
oh please, may your wise heart come back to its place,
where you put it!
In God's hands, in God's lap you put it,
which is the brightest hope;
but now, why does it descend and fall
into the abyss of despair?

QUEEN: I admit my mistake,
and my heart weeps for it,
but the pain that torments me erases
any possible good from my memory,
and my unhappy life
moves from pain to pain,
painfully,
so much so that no memory or faith
is left in me of good, or hope.[43]
But let not this mistake add to my offences:
may my soul rise, and you help it,
oh King who created it,
oh King of my life!
And if my limbs were dragged,
for my fault, into the darkness of sorrow,
may your pity lift up my soul

CAMERIERA: Ohimé, che sento!
e tu che dici, o mia reina! Torni,
torni 'l tuo saggio cor, dove star suole,
dove tu 'l riponesti!
In mano, in grembo a Dio tu 'l riponesti,
ch'è vivissima speme:
or, perché scende o cade
in disperati abissi?

REINA: Riconosco l'errore,
e già ne piange il coro;
ma 'l mal, che preme, a la memoria toglie
il ben, che può venir, e ne la vita
infelice ch'io passo,
provo che male a male
malamente succede,
tal ch'io non ho di ben né di speranza
più memoria né fede.
Pur, non s'aggiunga anco l'errore al danno:
sollevisi quest'alma, e tu l'aita,
o Re, che la cercasti,
o Re de la mia vita!
E se per colpa mia cadder le membra
in tenebroso affanno,
s'alzi per tua pietà l'anima almeno

43 In these lines, spoken with vivid directness and lacking her customary verbal flourish, the Queen appears as profoundly human.

and harbour it in your sweet serenity!	nel tuo dolce sereno!
LADY-IN-WAITING: May God hear these voices, and may	CAMERIERA: Ascolti Dio le voci, e loro impetri
his immense goodness afford them grace and mercy:	grazia e mercé la sua bontade immensa;
may he not blow the hope of freedom alone,	né spiri sol di libertà la speme,
but send us something good as well!	ma ci mandi anco il bene!
And for the disconsolate soul	E perché abbia conforto
to get comfort	anco da cose umane
also from human things,	l'anima sconsolata,
allow me, my queen, to return	concedi, o mia reina, ch'io ti torni
to your lament-flooded memory	a la memoria, scorsa in lamentarsi,
the man who led you here	quel che qui ti condusse
from the secluded chambers.	da le stanze riposte.
QUEEN: I remember him	REINA: Men soviene
and look if I see	e miro se pur veggio
approach the fortress door the soldier	mover di vêr la porta de la rocca
who among the many	il soldato, che sol, fra tanti e tanti
who serve as shelters and walls to this infirm woman	che fanno argine e muro a questa inferma
and prevent her escape,	a vietarle la fuga,
took pity on my shameful state	fatto pietoso del mio danno indegno,
and tries to help me.[44]	d'aiutarmi procura.
Yesterday he promised	In su quest'ora ieri
to come here about this time, but he's not here.	promise ei di venir, né pur appare.
I pray that some unfortunate accident did not	Deh, che qualche accidente non recida
put an end to his compassionate care!	la sua pietosa cura!

44 The kindness of others, including those that should be her enemies, is a testament to Mary's righteousness and to the injustice of her condition.

LADY-IN-WAITING: If you please, I will stay longer and wait for him, for it is suspicious if you do. Your being here such a long time seems to me unsafe and damaging. There may be someone who sees us unseen, and by making guilty people become more suspicious we might hinder our chances of receiving help.	CAMERIERA: Se commandi, poiché per tôr sospetto a te non lece, passerò io più oltre o aspetterollo. Ma star qui tu sì lungamente, parmi malsicuro e dannoso. Forse v'è chi ci vede, e nol veggiamo, e l'accrescer sospetti a gente ria può poi ne l'avenir chiuder la via a mille aiuti e mille.
QUEEN: This is true. But in this place I am allowed to breathe fresh air, and the more or less I stay here should not raise suspicion. Still, if there is any doubt that this might happen, let us keep our plans safe: I will leave.[45] You wait here, and if he comes, you already know what I'd like to know from him.	REINA: È ragion vera; ma questo luogo pur mi si concede per respirar al cielo, e più o meno ch'io vi stia, non devrebbe far sospettar altrui; pur, se v'è il dubbio, com'è possibil forse, assicuriamo l'opra, e io men vado. Tu qui aspetta: e se viene, già sai quel ch'io vorrei saper da lui.
LADY-IN-WAITING: I know, and am keen to fulfil your needs, as a humble faithful servant should.	CAMERIERA: Sòllo, e ho anco cura d'adempier quel che vuoi, come conviensi a fedel serva umìle.
QUEEN: Rather, as a wretched companion in misfortune and pain.	REINA: Anzi, pur come a misera compagna di sventure e d'affanni.

45 Mary has still not given up on the possibility that her liberation might indeed be accomplished.

LADY-IN-WAITING: Wretched, yes, but content,
for fate chose me,
my sweet queen,
to be your consort
in your harsh fate;[46]
and of the fatal yoke,
too shameful and heavy
for your beautiful royal neck,
I carry that part
which a heart full of faithfulness,
full of love can carry.[47]
May calm winds never blow,
nor sun shine,
nor water ever spring, if not salty,
for those who leave their friends
among the evils of a harsh fate,
and only in good times
give them their treacherous, unworthy affection.
But may lightning strike from a just heaven,
and the earth gape wherever those
who abandon their lawful prince,
to whom faithfulness and service are due
even crownless,
stamp their footstep![48]

CAMERIERA: Misera, sì, ma misera contenta,
poiché sorte m'elesse,
o mia dolce reina,
ad esserti consorte
ne la tua acerba sorte,
e del giogo fatale,
ch'è troppo indegno e grave
al bel collo reale,
sostengo io quella parte,
che sostener può cuore,
colmo di fedeltà, colmo d'amore.
Né mai placida spiri
aura, né sol risplenda
ned acqua sorga mai, se non amara,
a chi fra i mali di fortuna acerba
lascia l'amico petto,
e solo al ben riserba
l'infido, indegno affetto;
ma folgore dal Ciel giusto discenda,
o 'l terren s'apra, ovunque l'orma imprime
chi legitimo prencipe abbandona,
cui fedeltade e servitù si deve
anco senza corona!

46 The female bond between Mary and the Lady-in-Waiting is again emphasized here, as well as in the preceding lines.

47 The words of the Lady-in-Waiting are, yet again, ominous. The "beautiful […] neck" will resurface during the Butler's narrative of Mary's execution, only this time depicted in the moment in which the blade cuts through it and blood gushes out. Besides this lexical foreshadowing, these lines by the Lady-in-Waiting reinforce another one of the central themes, which is that of female companionship, friendship, and faithfulness.

48 The theme of faithfulness is further explored here, with particular emphasis on the relationship between masters and servants: this is an oblique reference to the perceived abandonment by the "rebellious, treacherous" Scots (v. 42), lamented by the Queen in her opening monologue. Subjects and servants are – or should be – equally bound to their sovereign.

But you, daughters,[49] what are you doing,
why are you coming out? Is the queen
alone in there?

CHORUS: She commanded us
to come outside in the open air, under the sky,
which we so rarely see; and she locked herself
alone in there, in the chamber furthest removed,
where she usually prays.[50]

LADY-IN-WAITING: May her prayers
give peace to her troubled soul! I will leave you now,
and walk to the point where
the warden allows
the prisoners' feet to wander;
I will be back here soon. Now, spend this hour,
given to you to breathe, by praising
God and praying, and let your tongues
accompany your affection: humble, devout
affection is needed for a great tragedy:
may the heavens show mercy.

Ma voi, figlie, che fate,
che tutte uscite? Resta dunque sola
la reina là entro?

CORO: Ella c'impose
il venircen qui fuori, a l'aria, al cielo,
che sì raro veggiam; e s'è rinchiusa
sola là, ne la stanza più riposta,
dove orar suole.

CAMERIERA: Impetrino i suoi prieghi
pace a l'alma affannata. Or qui vi lascio,
e darò un giro sin dove è permesso
dal capitan custode
che 'l prigioniero piè scorra ed arrivi:
fra poco qui ritorno. Voi quest'ora
datavi a respirar, spendete, prego,
lodando Dio e pregando, e accompagni
la lingua il vostro affetto: umil affetto
e devoto conviensi a gran sciagura,
ch'alfin si piega il Cielo.

49 The "daughters" are the damsels who, as in the tradition of Greek tragedy, appear as the Chorus.

50 The Chorus immortalizes Mary in her most emblematic stance, one that will come back at the end: her retreat into prayer.

CHORUS: Neither tongue nor heart
were ever too tired
for such necessary endeavour
among the terrible horrors of this misery.
Immutable, motionless,
enshrouded by a luminous veil
of white haze, the high Mind
is seated, where He judges
what happens and roams.
And the ancient quill of eternity
engraved the law in the hardest
diamond, which regulates
what shines above,
and transpires down here.
But if a humble soul with pure will
prays and sighs,
the voice shakes the heavens
and imperiously orders
the great decree which turns
to those who call and pray.[51]
Such law onto itself
did the high, infinite Power prescribe,
which, undefeated against mortals,
finds joy and glory
in granting victory to a shadow of itself.
Hear, oh immense Piety,
these ancient prisoners,
for whom You remain the last shelter.
Have mercy, oh great King,

CORO: Non fu stanca giamai
né la lingua né 'l cuore
ad opra sì devuta,
in tanto di miserie acerbo orrore.
Immutabile, immota,
in luminoso velo
di candida caligine s'asside
l'alta Mente, onde pende
quanto stassi e s'aggira,
e de l'eternità l'antico stile
in diamante durissimo la legge
impresse, onde si regge
quel che là su risplende
e quel che qua giù spira:
ma se prega e sospira
aggiunta a pura voglia anima umìle,
la voce il Ciel percuote
e imperiosa scuote
il gran decreto, che si volve e piega,
ov'è chi chiama e prega.
Tal legge a sé prescrisse
Potenza alta, infinita,
ch'essendo invitta contra quanto ha vita,
in dar ad un sospir di sé vittoria
si compiace e si gloria.
Odi, o Pietade immensa,
antiche prigioniere,
a cui Tu sola per rifugio resti;
d'infelice reina,

51 The juxtaposition of the higher plane of God and the lower plane of humans is stressed here by the Chorus: every act on earth is the direct consequence of divine determination.

upon an unhappy queen!	o gran Re, miserere!
And if you gave her the sceptre,	E s'a lei scettro desti,
oh powerful, oh just, oh pious,	o forte, o giusto, o pio,
let not her liberty be taken	libertà non le tolga
by the unjust and guilty orders	imperio ingiusto e rio
of an impious, evil will.[52]	d'empio voler maligno.
Oh merciful, oh benign One,	O pietoso, o benigno,
help us in our pains,	soccorri ai nostri danni,
and let victory be mine	e di guerra crudel fra tanti affanni
in this cruel war,[53] amid all suffering:	sia la vittoria mia;
may the merit be Yours!	il merto a te si dia!
But here comes one of our enemies,	Ma di là vien a lungo passo e lieve.
with long and light steps:	un de' nostri nemici:
alas, let him not come	misera me, non venga
as the bearer of new worries	autor di nuove cure
in our misfortunes!	a le nostre sciagure!
SERVANT: Women, who will take me where I can talk	SERVO: Donne chi mi conduce ov'io ragioni
to your queen? Where is she?	a la vostra reina? Ove si trova?
Is she among you?	O forse è qui tra voi?
CHORUS: She is not here, but cannot be	CORO: Qui non è, ma lontana
very far. Her fate prescribes her	esser molto non può. La sua fortuna
a small space. What do you want?	picciol cerchio le ascrive. Tu che chiedi?
Why such haste?	Che porti frettoloso?
SERVANT: I am sent to her	SERVO: A lei mi manda
by my master, who is the captain jailkeeper[54]	il mio signor, ch'è capitan custode

52 While Mary is a rightful, pious, anointed queen, Elizabeth – who is depersonalized as only a "will" ("voler") – is unjust and evil, not least because her political power is illicit and is divested of God's sanction.

53 These lines reinforce the idea that Mary sees herself as involved in nothing other than a holy war between orthodoxy and heresy, originating in the personal struggle between the two women and sovereigns.

54 Possible reference to Amias Paulet (1532–1588). The jailer appears as a character (Pauleto) in Gisberti's *La barbarie del caso* (1664).

of this prison and of the people who are gathered around it.	di questa prigion vostra e de le genti, che vi fan siepe intorno.
CHORUS: A sorry task!	CORO: Ufficio acerbo!
SERVANT: But to rule is sweet. Hurry, I need to speak to the queen.	SERVO: Ma dolce è 'l comman-dar. Su tosto, i' debbo parlar a la reina.
CHORUS: Here comes the Lady-in-Waiting: talk to her.	CORO: Qui vien la cameriera: a lei ragiona.
LADY: My friend, you can tell me what you must tell her, and I will report it to her at once.	CAMERIERA: Amico, a me puoi dire quel che dir devi a lei, e io ben tosto gliel'andrò a riferir.
SERVANT: I don't care if I talk to you or her: let her know that the captain warns her that royal ministers have come: great men, among the greatest in the kingdom.[55]	SERVO: Nulla m'importa parlar teco o seco: sappia solo che 'l capitan l'avisa che venuti son ministri reali, uomini eccelsi, dei maggiori del regno.
LADY: And why should my queen care about their arrival? They may stay or leave, as they please.	CAMERIERA: E ciò, ch'importa a la reina mia? Se son venuti, tornino o stien, come a lor pare.
SERVANT: I believe they can do that.	SERVO: Io credo che così possan far.
LADY: If only I could do	CAMERIERA: Così potesse

55 The ministers sent by Elizabeth to read Mary her orders and ultimately pronounce her death warrant.

the same with my other people!

con altri chi t'ascolta!

SERVANT: Different fates,
different power. But you look at me
and hear me with contempt,
while I bring you news
that is sweet and positive to hear.

SERVO: A varie sorti
vario è 'l poter: ma tu par che sdegnosa
mi rimiri e ascolti;
e pur apporto cose
dolci e care ad udirsi.

LADY-IN-WAITING: The soul, embittered by pain,
paints bitter images, either in voice,
in actions, or in behaviour; and habit
often trumps will.[56] Let this excuse
my words and acts, which may sound
or look bitter, but my mind
is not such towards you.

CAMERIERA: L'anima inacerbita dal dolore
forma imagini acerbe o ne la voce,
o negli atti e nei modi; e il costume
vince spesso la voglia. Ciò discolpi
il mio parlar, che forse amaro sembra;
o 'l sembran le maniere,
ma contra te non è già tal la mente:

Suffering and pain
darken my frowns.
Pray, what do you bring?

il fastidio, l'affanno
fronte ritrosa fanno.
Ma che apporti, ti prego?

SERVANT: The captain
sends me to the queen.

SERVO: A la reina
mi manda il capitan.

LADY-IN-WAITING: You have already said this.

CAMERIERA: Già ciò detto hai.

SERVANT: And the earls are here,
I don't know which ones, but four or five of them.

SERVO: E son venuti i conti, i' non so quali,
ma quattro o cinque sono...

LADY-IN-WAITING: Go on:
what does the captain say?

CAMERIERA: Segui il resto:
che però dice il capitan?

56 Here, the Lady-in-Waiting speaks as if she were the Queen herself: so deep is the connection between the two women that their souls are almost one and the same.

SERVANT: He believes,
and heard, that they may
be bringing with them
the order to set your queen free.[57]

SERVO: Ch'ei stima
e ha sentito cose, onde si puote
congetturar che rechin ordin seco
di liberar la tua reina.

LADY-IN-WAITING: Oh most delightful,
beloved voice,
yet unhoped for!

CAMERIERA: O voce
soavissima, amata
quanto poco sperata!

SERVANT: And for your hope,
the captain sends me to the queen
bearing this welcome news.[58]

SERVO: E perché speri,
mi manda il capitan a la reina
con la cara novella.

LADY-IN-WAITING: If this is true,
the captain may expect great reward,
since with this kind, merciful gesture
he gives the queen
that sweet comfort
which had long died in her heart!

CAMERIERA: Deh, s'ella fie mai vera,
alta mercé n'aspetti il capitano,
che con cortese ufficio, anzi pietoso,
affretta a la reina
quel soave conforto,
che nel suo cuor già lungamente
è morto!

Nor will you go unthanked,
oh beloved bearer
of most welcome good news.
The title of servant,
harsh to hear,
harder to feel,
will be taken away from you, I swear!
You will be served by people
better than those you served.[59]

Né tu sarai senza mercé devuta,
amato apportatore
di novelle amatissime e soavi:
il titolo di servo,
duro e grave a sentirsi,
durissimo a provarsi,
ti fie tolto, te 'l giuro!
E serviranno a te forse migliori
degli avuti signori.

57 The deception of impending liberation is finally realized by the Servant's misguided words.

58 Again, the Servant keeps the subject of hope going so that, from a dramatic viewpoint, the eventual revelation of its actual meaning might be even more powerful.

59 The promise is of earthly reward, the only kind that the Servant can conceive.

My queen is generous and thankful,
and will be even more so, since she has learned herself
how heavy is the weight
of an adverse fate.

È liberal la mia reina e grata,
e più 'l sarà, quanto in se stessa ha appreso
come sia grave il peso
di sorte sventurata.

SERVANT: Stirred by zeal,
I rushed my steps as much as I could.
But it wasn't duty
to my master that stirred me,
as much as my desire to let the queen
hear this news, which I believe
will be very dear to her.

SERVO: Io da buon zelo spinto
ho affrettato a mio poter il passo,
né tanto m'ha spronato
la servitù devuta al mio signore,
quanto 'l desio di far che la reina
sentisse tal novella; la qual stimo
che cara le sarà.

LADY-IN-WAITING: Oh, how dear it will be!

CAMERIERA: E quanto cara!

SERVANT: That's why I would like
to tell her myself; and besides,
I have more to say, which will be
equally sweet to hear.

SERVO: Però venir vorrei
io stesso a riferirla, oltra che anco
altro ho da dir, che altrettanto fie
caro ad udirsi.

CHORUS: Why don't you speak? Alas!
Why do you split the good,
by keeping for yourself things that don't benefit you
but would lessen my pain?

CORO: E perché 'l taci, lassa!
Perché dividi 'l bene,
di cui quel che ritieni a te non giova
e 'n me scema le pene?

SERVANT: My will and duty
both lead me to the queen.
Still, to tell you what you ask me
in the short time I have,
know that we believe for certain
that your king is so armed
and powerful that if our queen

SERVO: M'affretta a la reina
l'obligo mio e la voglia;
pur, perché breve spazio
fie lungo assai a dir quel che mi chiedi,
sappi che fra noi tiensi e s'ha per fermo
che 'l vostro re sia armato,
e sì forte, che quando la reina

does not do what he demands	nostra non sia per far di propria voglia
by freeing his mother,	quel ch'egli chiede, in liberar la madre,
she will be made to do so.	forse 'l farà cacciata da la forza.
This is the rumour among us, but those who speak	Questo fra noi si dice; ma chi 'l dice
do so quietly. Fear	sol fra le labra parla: la paura
is the mistress of silence. Nevertheless,	è maestra al silenzio. Io, pure, a voi
I did not want to conceal this from you	tacer non l'ho voluto: il compiacervi
pleasing you will benefit me.	so ch'utile mi fie.
CHORUS: If I could do	CORO: Così potessi
what I should, how certain	quel che poter devrei, come sarebbe
your belief would be!	certa la tua credenza!...
LADY-IN-WAITING: I will now go inside	CAMERIERA: Or io me n'entro
bearing two good pieces of news,	con due care novelle,
source of two hopes.[60]	fonti di due speranze.
I will go to her. You can follow me,	Io me ne vado a lei: tu puoi seguirmi,
my friend, if you so please, and you will be	amico, se ti pare, e tu sarai
the messenger and speaker. I cannot	il nunzio e 'l relator. Io non ti debbo
begrudge you the good that you can expect	invidiar il ben ch'aspettar puoi
from your sweet task, although my report	del caro ufficio tuo, benché bastante
would be enough to assure you	fôra il mio riferir, per conseguirti
the thankfulness you deserve.	la mercé, che n'aspetti.
CHORUS: He well deserves it!	CORO: Ei ben la merta!
Now go, my friend,	Or tosto vanne, amico,

60 The two hopes are, as the Servant has declared, that Elizabeth might by her own accord let Mary go or that King James might force her to do so by taking arms against her.

follow the Lady-in-Waiting; she enters the chambers.
With you both
in that unhappy place –
no, in my noble queen's bosom –
may that blissful happiness
enter, which never did,
since the day she was enclosed there:
that wretched woman,
who is the seat and pillar of all our happiness.
Leave the golden stars,
oh pure, winged, smiling,
dear hope,[61]
sweet honey for the afflicted mind,
and awaken pleasure where pain
resides in my queen!
To you I speak, oh hope,[62]
to you, sweet, useful, dear relic,
relic of that bitter jar[63]
whence the seed is spread
(if the old saying is true)
to the fields of life,
or rather, the cruel fruit of all evil.
Wretched mortals,
look where we were led by the unusual will
of too daring a woman!
But you, sweet, welcome
medicine against all pains,

segui la cameriera; ella se n'entra.
Entri con ambi voi
ne l'infelice albergo,
anzi nel sen de l'alta mia reina,
quel placido contento,
che non v'entrò giamai
dal dì che fu rinchiusa
la sconsolata donna,
ch'è d'ogni nostro ben seggio e colonna.
Movi da l'auree stelle
chiara, alata, ridente,
o cara lusinghiera,
o miel soave de l'afflitta mente,
e 'l piacer desta, ove 'l dolor si cria
ne la reina mia!
A te parlo, o speranza,
a te, dolce reliquia utile e cara,
reliquia di quell'urna acerba, amara,
onde 'l seme si sparse
(s'antico dir ha fede)
nei campi de la vita,
anzi 'l frutto crudel di tutti i mali.
O miseri mortali,
ove ci trasse curiosa voglia
di donna troppo ardita!
Ma tu, dolce, gradita,
medicina soave d'ogni doglia,

61 In the original, the subject of this apostrophe (hope) is not explicit ("o cara lusinghiera") and left implied for four more lines.

62 A powerful prosopopoeia.

63 The reference here is to Pandora's box (which was actually a large jar in the original Greek). Hope was the only element left in the box before it was again closed.

fly with fast wings
and bring comfort to the royal heart
where happiness has died.[64]

scendi con rapide ali,
e 'l cor regio conforta,
ove letizia è morta.

SERVANT: Lucky me, if the news I bring
comes true! I will go back
so full of hope and promises
that I have nothing else to wish for, if not the effects
of what the captain ordered me to say.
Oh, how generous, how courteous,
how sublimely grave and wise
is the queen I leave, and how unworthy
of such misery! How true it is
that where valour grows, fortune diminishes,
and that the best souls
get the worst fates!

SERVO: Felice me, se giunge ad esser vera
la portata novella! I' men ritorno
sì carco di speranze e di promesse,
che nulla ho da bramar, se non l'effetto
a quanto il capitano a dir mi diede.
Oh, com'è liberal, com'è cortese,
com'è soavemente e grave e saggia
la reina ch'io lascio, e quanto indegna
di sì misero stato! Ahi, pur è vero
ch'ove cresce valor scema ventura,
e ch'a l'alme migliori
giran sorti peggiori!

CHORUS: Fate mixes things
in an invisible jar,[65]
and then pours the good mingled with evil
in the mortal world.
Thus, if it gives someone
gifts of a noble aspect or intellect,
their fates are mixed with good and evil

CORO: Mesce le cose il fato
in invisibil urna,
e versa poscia il ben sparso di male
ne lo stato mortale.
Così, se porge altrui
doni d'alta presenza o d'intelletto,
con l'uno e l'altro è mista

64 This longing for hope problematizes the Queen's path to martyrdom: this wish is further proof that, by this stage in the tragedy, she is still more an earthly woman than a sacrificial lamb.

65 The reference to the jar comes back, but this time without the classical implication of Pandora's box.

which afflicts the soul.
To lesser people
the skies are blessed
with happy success.
Some lack valour
but abound with skill;
others have deceptive ideas
that are powerful and daring.
Thus in the varied faces
of murky, fickle nature,
nothing is free of misfortune,
nothing is free of fault:
happy are those
for whom good and bad
are balanced equally.[66]
Alas, the bitter and painful part
weighs too much
upon my queen!
Too, too unbearable is a pain
of twenty years!
But you, how did you find her?
How is she in there?
Did she find comfort and solace
in the good news?[67]

SERVANT: I entered, as you saw, and a dark
solitary staircase – how unworthy
of a royal guest! – led me to the upper chambers,
trailing behind that weak old lady
who left this place. There, past
the great hall and then the other one,
my guide stopped me and said: "Wait here,

sorte che l'alma attrista;
ad altri accorti meno
con felici successi
si volge il ciel sereno.
Ad un manca l'ardire
e soprabonda l'arte;
altri forte e audace
ha consiglio fallace;
così nel vario aspetto
de la natura torbida e incostante,
nulla è senza sciagura,
nulla è senza difetto,
e felici coloro,
a' quai con lance eguale
si parte il bene e 'l male.
Ma troppo, ahimé, s'avanza
ne la reina mia
la parte acerba e ria!
Troppo, troppo è un affanno
giunto al ventesim'anno!
Ma tu, come la lasci?
Come resta là entro?
È consolata, è lieta
con la novella lieta?

SERVO: Entrai, come vedeste, e fosca scala
solitaria, ahimé quanto, e quanto indegna
di regio albergo, a le sovrane stanze
mi trasse, dietro a quella debil vecchia,
che di qui si partì. Quivi passata
la maggior sala e quinci l'altro albergo,
mi ferma la mia guida e: — Qui m'aspetta,

66 Unlike Mary, in whose life the bad has far outweighed the good.

67 Gerato remarks that the use of *settenari* in the Chorus' speech conveys the accelerated rhythm of hopefulness ("Un'anima Traviata," 10).

I will be back."[68]	dice, ch'or qui ritorno. —
Then with a key	Indi con una chiave,
that hung from her side, she opened a door,	ch'al lato le pendeva, ha un uscio aperto,
entered, and closed it. But before	ed entrata il riserra: ma sì tosto
she did, there the queen	non l'ha potuto far, che colà entro
appeared before me,	non mi si sia scoperta la reina,
kneeling on the bare floor	che ginocchion premea lastrico nudo
with no cushion or rug, and her eyes	senza coscin, senza tapeto, e gli occhi
were fixed upon a cross hanging from the wall.[69]	fissi alti in una croce al muro appesa.
CHORUS: She keeps her eyes on the insignia	CORO: Gli occhi tien a l'insegna
and her heart for the captain,[70]	e 'l core al capitano,
and her soul is ready to fight for him,	e a pugnar per lui l'anima è accinta,
though her hand be weak.	benché debil la mano.
SERVANT: Once the old lady entered,	SERVO: La vecchia entrata dentro,
I heard another sigh, and then the door	sento un alto sospiro, e quinci a poco
slowly opened again, and thence the queen came out,	si riapre quell'uscio e 'n vista grave
sombre but with tranquil eyes,	e con occhi tranquilli, ancorché cinti
though red-rimmed	di purpureo color e molli ancora
and still wet from past tears, and she stopped	de le lagrime scorse, esce, si ferma
and looked at me.[71] In deepest	la reina e mi mira. Io, riverente

68 The way in which the Lady-in-Waiting is portrayed, and the lexical choice "guide" ("guida"), almost echo the figure of Virgil in the *Divine Comedy*: the ultimate sight, though, is that of the praying Queen.

69 From this moment on, Mary's transformation into the sacrificial victim starts taking clearer shape. These lines provide a visually incisive and intimate portrait of the Queen.

70 The captain ("capitano") is God.

71 After the previous image of rapt religious devotion, now Mary displays signs of humanity.

reverence, I bowed to her, and she said: "Friend,
why are you here? What news
does the captain send me?" "Happy news –
I replied – noble queen, as you can see
on my face, if your royal eyes can look this low."
Then I told her everything: that the earls
have arrived, why it is presumed they are here,
that her son is taking up arms, just as I told you.
She listened to me sombrely and without showing
any emotion. At last, seeing that
I wasn't speaking anymore, she turned her eyes
heavenward and said: "Glory to God!
May his will be done.[72] But you, my friend,
go back to the captain and greet him
in my name and tell him that
I thank him for his good work
in such a way
as only a disgraced woman can.[73]
Still, I give whatever I can, in the hope
of one day showing how beneficial it is

quanto più so, l'inchino, ed ella: — Amico,
a che vieni? — mi dice — o quai novelle
mi manda il capitan? — Liete, — rispondo, —
alta reina, e nel mio volto il vedi,
se così basso mira occhio reale. —
Quinci tutto le narro: e come i conti
son qui venuti, e a che fin si stimi,
e 'l figlio armato, come ho detto a voi.
Ella grave m'ha udito e senza segno
d'interno movimento: alfin, veggendo
ch'io più nulla dicea, gli occhi ha rivolti
in verso 'l ciel, e: — Gloria — dice — a Dio!
Poi seguane che vuol. Ma tu ritorna,
amico, al capitan, e a mio nome
il saluta cortese e digli ch'io
del suo benigno ufficio
quelle grazie gli do, che dar gli puote
donna di grazie priva.
Pur, quanto posso, do con voglia viva
di mostrar anco un dì, quanto a sé giovi

72 The Queen places all trust in God's plan, whatever it may have in store for her.
73 She insists upon her self-portrayal as an unhappy woman who fell from power and honour to disgrace through no fault of her own.

to one's self to be good to others, and even more
when one works for royal blood, which
is generous and giving by nature.[74]
To you, if ever I can, I will give
what you cannot hope for in your current
uneasy state. A great palace
and fields and woods for your enjoyment
will be my gifts.[75] Meanwhile, let this promise
be my thanks, and cherish this hope,
if someone whose only hope is in heaven
can ever give you one on earth."
With such sweet voice and goodly
ways she uttered her words.
And I, overwhelmed by sound and sight,
barely knew what to say, barely answered,
or perhaps said nothing.[76]

CHORUS: Royal presence stirs
wonder and awe in people's bosoms.
I wish you had seen her
seated on her noble throne,
amid all luxuries,

chi giova altrui, e più quando s'impiega
l'opra in sangue real, che per se stesso
benignamente è liberale e dona.
A te, s'io posso mai, sarà mercede
quel che sperar non puoi ne la fortuna
angusta, ove ti trovi: alto palagio
e larghi campi e selve a tuo diletto
ti fien mio dono. Intanto la promessa
ti sia mercede, e godi la speranza,
se speranza può dar d'opra terrena
chi per sé sol l'ha in Cielo. —
Con sì soave voce e sì benigne
maniere espresse ha queste sue parole,
ch'io, confuso dal suono e da la vista,
poco sapea che dir, poco ho risposto,
e nulla forse ho detto.

CORO: Stupor e riverenza
desta nei petti altrui real presenza:
ma se l'avessi vista
in ricco seggio assisa
fra le pompe lucenti,

74 Clearly, the anointed sovereign's nature will never relinquish her.

75 The fantasy of future retributions and future scenarios of bliss will come back later, not just in the words of the queen.

76 The "wonder and awe" ("stupor e riverenza") caused by the presence of royal greatness, as the Chorus will immediately determine. Sartorio Loschi's *Letter* (Appendix) touches upon this very effect as well.

when her youth
was still untouched by her pains:

oh, what superb sight of delight she was![77]
Oh, what painful memory!
However, the clouds of evil
clouded her royal looks,
but did not conceal them.

SERVANT: A flower shows
its morning hues
at melancholy dusk.[78]
I will go now, as my staying here
does you no good, and could hurt me.
Service requires
readiness: he who gets late to his master,
gets there in danger.[79]

CHORUS: Let our friendship not disappear,
though you may be gone.
Come back and see us, and tell us

what you hear: we are lonely and disconsolate,
and can only forget our grave concerns
by hearing new things.

SERVANT: I will do all I can for your benefit
that does not endanger me. But here comes

allorché 'l fior degli anni
tocco non era ancor dai duri affanni,
ahi, che vista era allor dolce e superba!...
Ahi, che memoria acerba!
Pur, il nembo dei mali
intorbidò, ma non oscura in lei
le sembianze reali.

SERVO: Del matutin colore
ne la languida sera
scopre imagine il fiore.
Or io men vo, ché la dimora mia
a voi non giova e a me nuocer potrebbe;
la servitù richiede
prontezza: al suo signor chi tardi arriva,
con suo periglio arriva.

CORO: Ma l'amistà non parta,

se ben si parte il piede.
Ritorna a rivederci, e quel che senti,
rapporta a noi, che sconsolate e sole
sol possiamo obliar le cure acerbe

col sentir nuove cose.

SERVO: Quel che senza mio rischio in util vostro
potrò adoprar, tutto farò. Ma ecco

77 A stark contrast to the wretched old woman kneeling before a crucifix.

78 This floral metaphor is also an omen of Mary's imminent end.

79 On the Servant's function in the tragedy, including in this moment of covert denunciation of the injustice of servitude to power, see Sanguineti White, *Dal detto alla figura*, 30–1.

the queen: my women, farewell!	che sen vien la reina: o donne, a Dio!
QUEEN: I hope, alas! Or should I not?[80] What should I make of the welcome, longed for news – both welcome and longed for – as against cruel evils mortals welcome dear, sweet hope?[81] It now shows itself to the heart from afar, and, yearning, it longs for it and stares, but the bosom is unable to give hope shelter. Enduring evil takes away the faith in the good that comes quickly!	REINA: Spero, lassa, o non spero? O che creder debb'io de la novella dolcissima bramata, dolce e bramata inseme, quanto fra i duri mali ai miseri mortali dolce e cara è la speme? La qual da lunge or si dimostra al core ed ei voglioso la vagheggia e mira, ma non sa l'arte il petto di darle in sé ricetto. La lunghezza del male toglie la fede al bene, che frettoloso viene!
LADY: Like a light morning dew, which bathes us unseen, comes what heavens devises for us, and most often we feel its effects before we see its signs.[82] But if we see the sign of good or evil, its reality must be more certain to us, like the thunder is more certain after we have seen the lightning.	CAMERIERA: Quasi lieve rugiada matutina, ch'invisibil ci bagna, vien quel ch'il Ciel destina, e più volte ne sentiam gli effetti, pria che vederne i segni. Ma se segno veggiam di bene o male, esser più certo a noi debbe il successo, quanto è più certo il tuono, poi che s'è visto il lampo.

80 Mary's humanity is testified by her timid indecisiveness on whether to accept the possibility of deliverance or not.

81 Hope is still the protagonist of this entire section.

82 A powerful simile is used to persuade the Queen to welcome hope in her heart.

QUEEN: But the sky often flashes,
and then goes quiet
and serene.
Similarly, the dawn often
appears before us,
but the sun does not.

REINA: Ma sovente balena,
e taciturno poi
il ciel si rasserena.
Così, spesso anco suole
apparirci l'aurora,
e poi non segue il sole.

CHORUS: Hope is such a common thing
that there is no human state
– misery, happiness, lowliness, haughtiness –
that eschews it.
Rather, sweet and benign,
it flies through the air of human things
both cloudy and serene,
and offers itself to the souls,
and generously donates itself
to whomever will take it.
And if hope resides
among the good things,
those who renounce the good,
renounce hope, too:
to such loss they add fault,
for it is a fault to give up
something which freely
gives itself to us with no effort.
Something that never hurts
and can only do well.

CORO: È cosa sì comune la speranza,
che non v'è stato umano,
o misero o felice, o vile o altero,
a cui ella si tolga.
Anzi pur soavissima e benigna,
per l'aria nubilosa o ver serena
dei vari avenimenti
volando, a l'alme s'offerisce e porge,
e di se stessa è donatrice larga,
ov'ha chi la riceva.
E se la speme ha luogo
fra le cose ch'han titolo di bene,
di bene anco si priva
chi di speme si priva,
e al danno congiunge anco l'errore;
s'è pur error privarsi
d'un ben, ch'a noi vuol darsi
senza fatica o prezzo,
d'un ben, che mai non nuoce
e può sempre giovarci.

QUEEN: As you say,
hope can fly and give itself to people;
but there is no point for it to fly and give itself
if no one sees it.
And the wretched can't see it among their pains,

REINA: Volar può la speranza,
come tu dici, ed offerirsi altrui;
ma nulla è ch'ella s'offerisca e voli,
se non v'è chi la veggia.
Né può vederla il misero fra i mali,

because the sum of their pains	ché la somma dei mali
obscures even the sight of good things,	l'imagine dei beni anco confonde
and shrouds heavens in a veil	e 'nvolve in cieco velo
invisible to their unhappy eyes.[83]	a l'infelice il cielo.
LADY: It seems to me that if hope	CAMERIERA: A me par, se la speme
is the expectation of something good,	è aspettazion di bene,
it befits the unhappy, since,	più si conviene a l'infelice, quanto,
by alternating the course	alternandosi il giro
of mortal things,	ne lo stato mortale,
evil takes the place of good,	il male al ben succede,
and good takes the place of evil.	e il ben succede al male.
We may therefore say	Quinci potrebbe dirsi
that hope for the unhappiest	che la speme del misero esser debbe
must be fear for the happiest.[84]	del felice la tema.
QUEEN: Do you want me to hope, then?	REINA: Vuoi tu dunque ch'io speri?
LADY: It is reason that wants it!	CAMERIERA: Anzi 'l vuol la ragione!
You also can't deny, my queen,	Né tu potrai negar, o mia rena,
that it does not behoove a great, royal soul	ch'a grande alma real non si sconvegna
to abandon your heart so fully to your pains,	lasciar il cor sì pienamente ai mali,
so much that no room is left for good,	che 'n sé non abbia loco almeno al bene
which comes from hope.	che da speranza viene.
If the news is true,	Se la novella è vera,
reason says: "Hope!"	la ragion dice: spera;

83 The decades of suffering have clouded the Queen's ability to foresee the possibility of good outcomes.

84 A beautiful chiasmus ("that *hope* for the *unhappiest* / must be *fear* for the *happiest*"; "che la *speme* del *misero* esser debbe / del *felice* la *tema*," my emphasis) punctuates the Lady-in-Waiting's reasoning.

If it is false,
how can hoping in vain
be any harm to us?
But forget reason, let the pleas
of these servants of yours be enough.
Comfort us, I beg you,
by showing us the sweet sight
of a happier face.
You are our sun and hope!
If there is no light or hope inside you
we can only be
in desperation and darkness.

QUEEN: May my soul be made to hope by your will,
since it will not by mine! I hope, my women![85]
And I believe that the spinning wheel,[86]
long hinged
to the spindle of my misfortunes,
is now moving upwards from the bottom,
if not to take me back to the place
of my previous life
– where I was born, where I was –
at least to make me breathe
fresh air, which gives nourishment and spirit and life
to those on earth.

CHORUS: May heavens grant you this;
your rights will lead and fight
for the rest.

se sarà falsa poi,
l'aver sperato invano,
che può nuocer a noi?
Ma non vaglia ragion, vagliano i prieghi
di queste serve tue:
consolaci, ti prego,
con la vista bramata
di fronte consolata!
Tu nostro sol, tu nostra speme sei:
se 'n te la luce e la speranza è sgombra,
noi solamente siamo
disperazione e ombra.

REINA: Speri l'alma al voler de l'altrui voglia,
s'al mio voler non puote! Io spero, o donne;
e vuo' stimar che la girevol ruota,
fissa già lungamente
col chiodo del mio danno,
or dal fondo si mova in vêr la cima,
se non per trarmi al seggio
de la fortuna prima,
ov'io nacqui, ov'io fui,
almen perch'io trar possa
l'aria, ond'han nodrimento e spirto e vita,
sotto libero cielo.

CORO: Ciò ti conceda il Cielo;
ch'a conseguir il resto
fia duce ed arme il dritto.

---

85 The Queen is finally, and tragically, persuaded.

86 The image of the wheel of fortune, evoked upon the Queen's first appearance, is again employed.

QUEEN: Oh, that I could
see again the fields
of my beloved homeland,[87]
of the kingdom where the long, ancient stream
of my glorious blood
ran amid sceptres and crowns;
where the ashes lie
of the many noble bones
which gave flesh to my tired flesh!
What shall I say? What shall I do? How shall I feel?
What shall I think?
These eyes of mine will see the eyes
of many loving people looking at me,
and will they see my joy
on many faces and in many voices.
I will honour and be honoured,
And be thankful for being served;
I will forgive and put people back
to their previous places.
I will hear and answer, offering
pardons and mercy.[88]
Oh, tasks long neglected,
both sweet and painful,
how you come back to my soul
with a little hope!

REINA: Oh, se fia mai ch'io giunga
a riveder i campi
de la mia patria amata,
del regno, ove già lungo, antico rivo
del sangue mio ben glorioso corse
fra scettri e fra corone;
ove 'l cenere giace
di tant'ossa onorate,
ond'ebber carne queste carni stanche,
che dirò? Che farò? Qual sarà il core?
Quai saranno i pensieri?
Vedran questi occhi gli occhi
di tante amate genti a sé rivolti
e la letizia mia
partita in mille fronti, in mille cori.
Onorerò onorata,
più gradirò servita;
perdonerò, tornerò il seggio a molti
de la prima fortuna;
ascolterò, risponderò, donando
or grazie ed or mercedi:
ahi, opre lungamente tralasciate,
come in lieve speranza
or fra dolci ed acerbe
a l'alma mi tornate!

CHORUS: Here comes a foreign-looking man,

CORO: Di colà viene uomo straniero in vista

87 This entire speech is again Mary's fantasy of a happy future, where she regains her past glory. Scotland, her homeland, takes centre stage in this projection of bliss.

88 As Sanguineti White remarks, this speech emphasizes the affective network of reciprocity between the monarch and her subjects, which is the symbol of good governance (*Dal detto all figura*, 25–6).

with an authoritative stride.[89]
I may have seen him other times,
or perhaps my weak sight is tricking me:
may God bring him here as a friendly star,
a messenger of dawn, of the sun,
of our freedom!

QUEEN: I know him,
he is a cruel acquaintance of old.
Yet I don't know what will happen now:
the sight of that face still pains me!

CHORUS: He is Beale, the counsellor
and friend of our enemy.
Perhaps as a remedy to his past
disdainful and haughty offences, he took the charge
of this gracious, dear task.

QUEEN: A vile, low soul
can hardly become noble.
Hush, he approaches. Or should I
go back inside? My heart shakes,
hurts, angers.

COUNSELLOR: Four horned moons
reached full circle around their complex path,

e 'n autorevol passo.
Forse altre volte l'ho veduto, o pure
m'inganna il debil occhio:
faccia Dio ch'egli venga amica stella,
messaggiera de l'alba, anzi del sole
de la libertà nostra!

REINA: Il riconosco,
e fu già un tempo conoscenza acerba;
non so quel ch'or sarà: quel volto ancora
m'affligge in rivederlo!

CORO: Egli è Beel, il consigliero, amico
de la nostra nemica.
Forse per sodisfar passata offesa
di disprezzo e d'orgoglio, ha preso il carco
d'esser ministro a cortese opra e cara.

REINA: Anima bassa e vile
mal può farsi gentile.
Tacciam, ch'egli s'appressa. O pur è meglio
ch'io men rientri. Il cor troppo si scuote,
s'addolora, s'adira.

CONSIGLIERO: Già quattro lune da l'acute corna
per l'intorto sentier son giunte al cerchio

89 The reverie is abruptly interrupted: after this long sequence of thoughts and dreams, action is bound to resume with the arrival of Elizabeth's emissary.

and formed different faces by waxing and waning,
since the time I was here,[90]
when I left you sombre and irate
with me, against the rightful orders
of my noble queen. I will blame it
on natural emotion – which makes us
focus on ourselves and often obscures our sense
of correct ideas – that you spoke
bitter, rough words against me
and my queen.[91] Now I am back
with a peaceful, tranquil soul;
and I seek to find
your mind bright and free
from lowly daze and emotions
which obfuscate clear reason.
My queen, moved by pain
for your misery, where you were brought
by your fault of wanting too much,
and by your obstinate, false opinions,
by which you took thousands and thousands of souls to the deepest abyss
of eternal darkness, sends me here.[92]

e 'n varii volti si son colme e sceme,
dal tempo ch'io qui venni, onde partimmi
lasciando te grave e sdegnosa troppo
incontra me, contra i decreti giusti
de l'alta mia reina. E si conceda
al natural affetto, che c'inchina
verso noi stessi e spesso toglie il senso
di vera opinion, che tu formassi
parole amare, acerbe ad onta mia
e de la mia reina. Or io ritorno,
torno con alma placida e tranquilla;
così anco ricerco
da te la mente luminosa e sgombra
da le nebbie comuni e dagli affetti,
che soglion oscurar la ragion chiara.
La mia reina, mossa da l'affanno
de le miserie tue, dove t'addusse
colpa di voler troppo ed ostinata
e falsa opinion, onde traevi
teco mill'alme e mille ai ciechi abissi
de le tenebre eterne, a te mi manda.

90 Astrological periphrasis: four months have passed since his last visit.

91 The Counsellor's tone is sneering from the very start.

92 The accusations are clear: the Counsellor is firmly on his queen's side and brazenly sings her praises as an introduction to the three damning requests to follow.

First, which is right and fair,
she demands and wants that the title of heir
to the Kingdom of England, which you claim
as your own, be taken from you and that you
negate it, renouncing the right
you claim by it;[93] then that you give up
the title of queen and leave the crown
and sceptre and royal mantle to your son:
so that he may rule and govern without you,
and you live as a subject to the laws
that the Council will impose, the Council
appointed by my queen.[94] She then wants you
to confirm the past things
done in Scotland, which were introduced
there by the new religion and the new worship
of the divine mystery, and promise
for yourself, your son, and the kingdom

E prima, com'è dritto e com'è giusto,
chiede e vuole che 'l titolo di erede
del regno d'Inghilterra, che presumi
a te deversi, ti sia tolto e sia
da te negato, rinunziando al dritto,
che 'n ciò pretendi; e quinci che ti spogli
del nome di reina e lasci al figlio
la corona e lo scettro e 'l regio manto,
sì ch'egli senza te regga e governi,
e tu viva soggetta a quelle leggi,
che 'l Consiglio imporrà; Consiglio eletto
da la reina mia. Poscia vuol anco
che tu confermi le passate cose
in Scozia fatte e già colà introdotte
con nuova religione e nuovo culto
nei misteri divini, promettendo
tu per te, per tuo figlio e per lo regno

93 The first demand is directly connected to Elizabeth's fears that Mary might claim the English throne.

94 The second demand has to do with the Kingdom of Scotland. By asking that Mary renounce her title and leave the throne to her son, the Counsellor implies that that is not yet the case. However, this is both incongruous with the rest of the tragedy's fictional reality (James is, in fact, spoken of as King of Scotland, not heir to the throne) and ahistorical, since Mary had been forced to abdicate almost twenty years prior (although she never ceased to consider herself queen).

that they will be observed entirely.[95]	ch'osservate saranno illese, intatte.
Moreover, as per holy rites,	Anzi, che quanto tocca ai sacri riti,
holy people, holy offices,	a le sacre persone, ai sacri uffici,
it will be done as will be the desire and law	tanto fie sol, quanto fie voglia e legge
of those who hold, or will hold, rightfully the title	di chi tiene o terrà titolo giusto
of king of England, knowing	di rege d'Inghilterra, conoscendo
only the royal seat of English kings	solo il seggio real dei regi inglesi
as the legitimate seat, whence the true authority	per legitimo seggio, onde proceda
of holy faith proceeds;	la vera autorità del sacro culto;
and let Rome be declared impious and fallacious	e si pronunzii Roma empia e fallace
for centuries to come to the Scottish kings	nei secoli avenir ai re scozzesi,
and people, and to Scotland as a whole.[96]	ai popoli, a le genti, a Scozia tutta.
I come here as a minister and this I bring you.	Tal ministro vengh'io: questo t'apporto,
My queen, a most merciful	e ciò ti manda la reina mia,
and powerful queen, sends this to you.	reina pietosissima e possente.
You choose and answer. I will be the messenger	Eleggi tu e rispondi. Io messaggiero
of your will to the five men appointed	sarò del tuo voler a cinque eletti
by the royal mind, who are already here	da la mente real, già qui condotti
with royal authority and royal sceptre,	con regia autoritade e regio scettro
to execute what will be right.	ad essequir quel che fie poscia giusto.

95 The third demand is the religious one, which, expectedly, will be the centrepiece of Mary's rebuttal.

96 Elizabeth's wild dream of the repudiation of Rome for all of Scotland is clearly intended as a provocation.

QUEEN: She who sends, he who comes, and what is said
are equally cruel: and what needs to follow
is similarly unjust. But if she who sends
and he who speaks are cruel, I am wretched
in listening, and more wretched yet
for my soul is harshly reminded
of the grave error that I made
when I put my faith in her, who
has no faith even in her Creator.[97] I was foolish then:
now I will be sentenced, I know.
Let it be what it may. You, who came here
to receive my words, listen and tell.
I must not and will not take away from myself
what God gave me.[98] He, in His mercy,
made me be born a queen: in dying,
He shall receive me as a queen. May the royal
sign follow my unbound soul. If she thinks
she can take it from me, let her come and take it!
To leave my kingdom to my son is a just
and welcome thing, but I will do so

REINA: E chi manda e chi viene e quel che dice,
egualmente è crudel: così fie ingiusto
quel che n'ha da seguir. Ma s'è crudele
e chi manda e chi parla, io che l'ascolto
misera son, e misera altrettanto,
quanto più vivo or mi ritorna a l'alma
il gravissimo error, commesso allora
ch'io diedi fede a chi la fede nega
anco a Chi la creò: fui sciocca allora;
or sarò condennata, i' me n'accorgo.
Ma sia che può. Tu ch'a ricever vieni
le mie parole, ascolta e riferisci.
Tôrre a me stessa quel che Dio mi diede,
né 'l debbo, né 'l consento. Ei, sua mercede,
nascer mi fe' reina: anco reina
mi riceva morendo. Il regio segno
segua l'anima sciolta: s'altri stima
di potermen privar, venga e 'l si tolga!
Lasciar il regno al figlio opra è devuta
e bramata anco, ma lasciarlo allora

97 Elizabeth is faithless both to humans (because she betrayed Mary) and to God (because she is a Protestant).

98 Mary reinforces the idea of her divine right: she was made a queen at birth, and she will die one, no matter what humans will do to her. Her words essentially denounce the emptiness of the second demand.

when God demands I leave both kingdom and life.[99]
And if he is wise
and strong like his ancestors, your queen
will want to make sure to keep
the Council for herself, without giving it to him.
Scotland is not so weak or foolish
not to be able to produce its own kings.[100]
That I claim to be heir to England
I will not deny: my blood, which makes me a lady
calls me to that kingdom. However, if
the people want me to give up
my right, I will give it up. Let them choose
a king of better ancestry, if they can find
one better than the Stuarts.[101]
But that I should confirm
the new faith
of religion in my kingdom,
or that I consent that it take sacred orders and rites
from anywhere other than the Roman seat,
is an impious demand,

ch'imporrà Dio ch'io lasci regno e vita.
E s'egli sarà saggio
e forte eguale agli avi, assai gran cura
avrà la tua reina in ritrovarsi
per sé 'l consiglio, senza darlo a lui;
né così imbelle è Scozia o così stolta,
che non basti a produr regi a se stessa.
Che d'Inghilterra erede i' mi pretenda,
negar nol voglio: il sangue, onde son donna,
a quel regno mi chiama. Pur, se fie
voler comun del popolo ch'io lasci
il mio dritto, ecco 'l lascio; egli s'elegga
re di stirpe miglior, se la ritrova
miglior de la Stuarda.
Ma ch'io confermi poi
il culto rinovato
de la religion del regno mio,
o ch'io consenta ch'egli prenda altronde,
fuor che del roman seggio, ordini e riti
nei sacri uffici, è empia la dimanda

99 Again, the inaccuracy is both factual and fictional, although it serves the theme of martyrdom, which is building ever more strongly throughout this exchange.

100 This might be Della Valle's nod to what was to indeed to happen (and had happened by the time the printed edition was published in 1628): it was the Scottish royal family who would become rulers of England, and not the other way around.

101 Mary skilfully shifts the perspective from a fight between peers (Elizabeth and her) to a broader consideration which brings into question the will of the people (*ius gentium*). In this way, she lets go of any direct role in the matter.

and the hope that I will accept it is foolish.[102]
And if my refusal has to be paid
with blood, here is my blood, and here is my throat.
I am not so bound to this life
or kingdom that I should desire one or the other
tainted by impiety![103] Tell these things
to those who must hear them. And also tell
your queen that it was the trust she promised me
that led me to this condition:

to hear unjust, impious demands,
to live a shameful life of captivity.
For she may deem me
a fool if I believed her,
but I have reason to deem her

cruel and deceitful.
These titles she should add to the noble
title of queen and to her name, Elizabeth,
instead of what she yearns for,
queen of Scots! I will now leave

with that little freedom which your queen
gives me: the freedom to enter
this unworthy dwelling, and then exit it
to breathe a little air.

e sciocca la speranza d'impetrarla.
E se 'l mio contradir ha da pagarsi
col sangue, eccoti 'l sangue, ecco la gola;
non sì amica son io di questa vita
o del regno, ch'io brami o l'una o l'altro
con l'empietà congiunta! Queste cose
rapporta tu a chi devi, e più, soggiungi
a la reina tua ch'a passo tale,

ch'a udir dimande niquitose ed empie,
a viver vita prigioniera e indegna,
m'ha tratto quella fé ch'ella mi diede:
però ch'ella me stimi
sciocca, se la credetti,
ché con ragion lei stimar posso e stimo
e perfida e spergiura.
Questi titoli aggiunga al titol chiaro
di reina e al nome d'Isabella,

e sian invece di quel ch'ella brama
di reina di Scozia! Or io men vado
con quella libertà, che sol mi lascia
la tua reina, di poter entrare
in questo indegno albergo e uscir poi
a trar l'aria a misura.

102 The moment to which the tragedy had been building up: Mary's profession of faith and fight against the corruption of heresy. As Franco Croce wrote, Mary is "a martyr of her fidelity both to the Roman Church and to the royal mission" ("martire della sua fedeltà alla Chiesa Romana e insieme della sua fedeltà alla missione regale," *Federico Della Valle*, 38).

103 She explicitly declares that she is ready for her blood to be shed: the theme of martyrdom has now been articulated.

COUNSELLOR: Leave! Here will soon come he who will curb the pride and royal grandeur of the lowliest of women.[104]	CONSIGLIERO: Vanne, ché qui verrà fra spazio poco chi la superbia domi e 'l regio fasto di bassissima donna!
LADY: A harsh reply to a cruel demand must not be deemed haughty. Those who seek that which they should not seek will find what they don't want to find.	CAMERIERA: A dimanda crudel, risposta acerba non si dica superba. Giusto è che chi ricerca quel che cercar non dee, trovi quel che non vuole.
COUNSELLOR: May words be equal to fate: those who serve and those who command have different things to say.	CONSIGLIERO: A la fortuna sian pari le parole: altro ha da dir chi serve, altro chi impera!
CHORUS: A great soul is only a servant to what is right, and such servitude is real power! But you, who see the injustice and wrongfulness (which you can't deny, if you have human reason) of your queen against my queen, you must concede that the pain of the offence may at least be channelled in her offended demeanour. Allow an imprisoned queen, grieved from twenty years of the harshest pain, to call cruel the woman who takes the kingdom from her,	CORO: Serva solo è del giusto anima grande, e servitute tale è imperio reale! Ma tu, che vedi l'ingiustizia e 'l torto (né già negar il puoi, s'hai senso umano) de la reina tua ver la reina mia, conceder déi che 'l dolor de l'offesa si sfoghi almen col dimostrarsi offesa. Consentasi a reina prigioniera misera di vent'anni in durissimi affanni, poter chiamar crudele chi del regno la priva,

104 The Executioner.

who keeps her captive.[105]
Don't speak, or – if you are so forced
by the job you came to do –
speak the true words,
but don't say the harsh ones!
A faithful minister
must benefit his master as much as he can,
but not harm others with what he sees
which, either revealed or concealed,
does not benefit his master;
the same things can be
sweet or bitter,
depending on how they are told.[106]

COUNSELLOR: It brings neither harm nor benefit if I speak or don't;
I did not come here so that
by your mistress's words
a new order would be pronounced
or that the existing one would be changed.[107]
The decision is made: what it is,
that haughty head,[108] which speaks magnanimously
and keeps her regality amid poverty,
will soon hear. I was sent here
merely to hear what I heard, and thus

chi la ritien cattiva.
E taci, o riferisci le parole,
le vere sì, s'a ciò ti sforza l'opra,
a cui mandato sei,
ma non ridir l'acerbe!
Deve fedel ministro
giovar quanto più puote al suo signore,
ma non nuocer altrui con quel che vede,
che, scoperto o taciuto,
al suo signor non giova;
e soavi, e acerbe
formar si ponno le medesme cose,
come son riferite.

CONSIGLIERO: Non nuoce o giova ch'io più dica o meno;
né venn'io qui, perché da le parole
de la padrona tua
ordin nuovo si fesse,
o si cangiasse il fatto.
Già è fisso il consiglio; e qual ei sia
ben tosto il sentirà la testa altiera,
che magnanima parla e 'l regio serba
fra le mendicità. Fui mandat'io
sol per udir quel che s'è udito e quinci

105 The Chorus tries to mitigate Mary's outburst, incapable of accepting that the Queen has cemented her death sentence.

106 On the figure of the "faithful minister" and the legacy of Baldassarre Castiglione's idea of the perfect courtier, see Sanguineti White, *Dal detto alla figura*, 32–3.

107 The Counsellor comes clean: the point was never to give Mary a chance, but rather to humiliate her if she were to give in.

108 This synecdoche has the effect of depersonalizing Mary and acts as a prelude to the scathingly mocking lines to follow. The Counsellor's cruelty is exaggerated almost to the point of caricature.

to confirm my queen's	confermar il giudicio e la sentenza
judgment and ruling.	de la reina mia:
And if the unfortunate woman were to answer differently,	e s'altro rispondea la sventurata,
and humiliate her proud soul,	umiliando l'anima superba,
laughter would be humility, and scorn	riso era l'umiltade e s'aggiungeva
would be added to punishment.	a la pena lo scherno.
CHORUS: What a cruel thought	CORO: Ahi, pensier crudo
from an evil soul!	e d'anima maligna!
COUNSELLOR: You can judge	CONSIGLIERO: A te si lasci
the cruelty or piety of our thoughts	giudicar con parole il crudo o 'l pio
with words. We will judge	dei pensier nostri: noi de l'altrui vita
her life with deeds.	giudicherem coi fatti.
CHORUS: Let the unjust, cruel hate	CORO: Sopra me si disfoghi
unload upon me, and let my blood	l'odio ingiusto e crudele, e il mio sangue
quench the greedy thirst	spenga l'ingorda sete
of that woman, or rather a Fury crowned	di donna, anzi di furia, coronata
with jewels on her head and serpents in her soul.[109]	di gemme il capo e l'alma di serpenti.
There goes the haughty minister	Sen va il ministro fiero
of a haughtier queen.	di reina più fiera,
And he brings in his mind the guilty venom	e porta ne la mente il rio veneno
(which he will exude from his mouth),	(e 'l trarrà per la bocca),
the deathly venom,[110] which heaven	il veneno morta, che già molt'anni

109 The reference is to Elizabeth, who is dehumanized and likened to a monster. On this passage, and more generally on the portrayal of the English queen, see Introduction, p. 18.

110 The venom that, in keeping with the previous image, originates from the serpents in Elizabeth's soul.

has been fortifying for many years!

QUEEN: You have heard the unjust demands,
my friends; and I know you have seen,
through your sorrow and pity
for my misfortune, the way they were asked.
What one expects is worse, if anything worse
remains among human evils, or if a cruel soul
can conceive yet something else to harm others.
And if death were to come late to me,
the reason is not pity, but cruelty.[111]
My twenty years of suffering are a short punishment
for the insatiable thirst
of the woman[112] who holds me captive: surely she saw me
as an enemy once, but now she keeps me for her amusement.
But may this be the fun of a cruel lion
who holds a little doe in his claws:
now he keeps her to his side, now he stops her
and turns her round, now he lets her free
for a couple of steps, and then attacks her
and seizes her: and finally he tears her apart,

ci va temprando il Cielo!

REINA: Udite avete le dimande ingiuste,
amiche, e la maniera di spiegarle,
so, con vostro dolor e con pietade
de la sventura mia, veduta avete.
Peggio è quel che s'aspetta, s'ancor peggio
resta fra i mali umani o s'altro ancora
può pensar alma cruda in danno altrui.
E se la morte forse a me sì tarda,
pietà non n'è cagion, ma crudeltade.
Breve pena è 'l mio danno di vent'anni
a l'insaziabil voglia
di chi mi tiene in forza; e certo m'ebbe
già per nemica un tempo, or m'ha per scherzo.
Ma scherzo fie d'aspro leon, che tiene
fra gli artigli cervietta;
ch'or la costringe al fianco, or la rallenta
e la volge e rivolge, or due o tre passi
sciolta la lascia e quinci a lei s'aventa
e ratto la ghermisce: alfin la squarcia

111 Mary's readiness for death, in this specific instance, is articulated in entirely earthly terms, rather than in metaphysical ones: here, she longs for death as release from her suffering rather than as testimony to her faith.

112 "A woman" is an explicit rendering of the Italian relative pronoun "chi," by which Della Valle keeps the subject of the sentence vague.

and fills his voracious throat with blood.[113]	e di sangue empie le voraci canne.
The unpredictable whirling of	Non si fermerà prima
this wheel[114] on the harsh battlefield	il vario raggirar di questa ruota
where my enemy keeps waging war on me	sul duro campo, ove la mia nemica
will not stop until	mi fa continua guerra,
my blood has become tragic ink	che ’l mio sangue sarà tragico inchiostro
for papers of sorrow.[115]	a dolorose carte,
And her cruelty	e l’altrui crudeltade
to my detriment will be at last celebrated	nel danno mio fie celebrata alfine
with horror and pity.[116]	con orror e pietade.
LADY-IN-WAITING: The inconstancy of your unstable state	CAMERIERA: Da l’incostanza del tuo vario stato
must be blamed upon those who trick you	argomentar si deve in chi t’aggira
into uncertain desires; and like a fever,	voglia indeterminata; e come febbre
which changes its course and strikes with varying strength,	che varia il corso e ’n furor vario assale,
is seldom deadly,	rare volte è mortale,
so we must hope	così anco debbiamo,
for release	ne l’aspra infermità de la tua sorte,
after the grave infirmity of your fate.[117]	sperar salute.

113 This metaphorical language further emphasizes the constrast between the two queens: one is voracious and violent like a lion (or a tiger, later), the other is vulnerable like a doe.

114 The wheel of fortune image returns yet again.

115 The first of two astoundingly metaliterary reflections, denoting both Della Valle’s writing in the martyrological tradition, as well as the broader fortune and resonance of the story.

116 The second metaliterary reflection, which focuses on audience reactions.

117 The Lady-in-Waiting is still ostensibly harbouring hope that her Queen might be released. The simile revolves around the noun “salute,” which can mean both health (as she intends it) and salvation (as the Queen does in the following lines): the English “release” appeared to be a sufficiently ambivalent, though not entirely synonymous, solution.

QUEEN: I hope for release, but of a different kind than you do. But what say you of the demands? What do you think?	REINA: Io la salute spero, non già qual tu la speri! Ma che dici de l'udite dimande? E che ne stimi?
LADY-IN-WAITING: The demands are cruel and unjust: who would not see that? But those who demand don't take away: and a harsh reply soothes the pain of those who hear harsh things. What I think is that your enemy sees herself threatened either by your son or by the Spanish king: and thus she tries to get what she can from you before, outpowered, she sets you free.	CAMERIERA: Crude son le dimande e sono ingiuste: e qual occhio nol vede? Ma chi chiama, non toglie, e la risposta acerba è medicina al dolor di chi ascolta acerbe cose. Or, quel ch'io penso e stimo, è che la tua nemica ora si veggia stretta da qualche rischio o per tuo figlio o per l'ispano re, e perciò tenta quel che può trar da te, pria che sforzata ti disciolga e sprigioni.
QUEEN: I believe she will set me free, but my soul will be freed before.[118]	REINA: Sprigionerammi, credo, ma a l'alma prima fia tolta la prigionia.
LADY-IN-WAITING: Alas, you torment my mind with dark omens! Your fear does nothing but damage you, my queen. You are asked to leave your son the crown and the kingdom; nothing is said	CAMERIERA: Misera me, con quai duri presagi mi tormenti la mente! Il tuo temere nulla val, se no al danno, o mia reina. A te si chiede la corona e 'l regno, che s'impieghi nel figlio; de la vita

118 Unlike her companion's, Mary's thoughts are beyond earthly hope.

about your life; and if the bold tongue of
the cruel minister threatens so, often the arrogance
of servants reaches farther than
the commands of masters; you know
who came, who spoke: a vile man,
lifted to great heights, is superb and insolent.
I will say more, my queen,
and I will say
what my soul truly feels.
This news,
which must be
in part true, the long span of our sorrows,
the changing fates – which must also turn
in our favour – and these demands, made at a time,
at a time, I say, when we know
our king is armed, and perhaps so is Spain,
against the evil woman who holds us prisoner,
reinvigorates my tired spirits
and the ailing blood of this heart battered
by years of suffering,
and strengthens my soul.
I hope[119] and believe, and I picture pleasant

si tace, o se minaccia audace lingua
di ministro crudel, talvolta scorre
l'arroganza servile ove non giunge
il signoril impero; e già conosci
chi venne, chi parlò: fortuna vile
inalzata è superba ed insolente.
Più dirò, mia reina,
e dirò veramente
quel che l'anima sente.
Queste udite novelle,
le quali esser denno
in qualche parte vere, il lungo corso
dei nostri mali, il variar del cielo,
che pur anco per noi debbe girarsi,
queste dimande poi, fatte a tal tempo,
al tempo, dico, che sappiam ch'armato
è 'l nostro re, e quel di Spagna forse,
contro la cruda ria che c'imprigiona,
ai miei languidi spirti, a l'egro sangue
di questo cor vinto da danni e anni
spiran vigor che mi rinforza l'alma.
E spero e credo, e imagino soavi

119 The Lady-in-Waiting gives in to the fantasy of an imminent future with Mary back on the Scottish throne: one last bout of hope before the impending doom of the Queen's life manifests in ways that even she cannot ignore.

times of delight; and I already see myself
in your chamber, my queen,
calling earls and dukes, and I see them leave
full of high hopes and thankfulness.
And I also see you seated
on a high throne, adorned with gems and gold,
backed by a host of armed men;
on one side, the beautiful group
of damsels and ladies on show,
rich in both garments and appearance;
and on the other side, in a sombre and majestic line,
hanging on your every word, excellent men
giving you their wisdom and advice.
And you, benevolent, receiving happy
congratulations and gifts from royal
messengers, brought to you from hence and thence
through long paths and from various places;
and hearing the humble requests
of your faithful people, of nobles and plebeians,
and granting some,
and denying others, according to the law
and what is right; but always sweet,

e dilettosi tempi; e già mi fingo
ne la camera tua, reina mia,
chiamar or conti, or duci, ed essi uscirne
lieti d'alte speranze e di mercedi.
Quinci anco te parmi veder assisa
in alto seggio ornato a gemme e oro,
cui faccian genti armate ampia corona,
e da un lato, vaghissima, la schiera
di damigelle e donne in varia mostra,
per abito ricchissime e per forma;
da l'altra, in grave e maestevol riga,
intenti ai cenni tuoi, uomini eccelsi
da la fronte spirar senno e consiglio;
e te benigna ora ricever liete
gratulazioni e offerte da reali
messaggier, quinci e quindi a te condotti
per lunghissime vie da varii lidi,
or ascoltar del popol tuo fedele,
di nobili e plebei, richieste umili,
e graziosa te conceder parte,
parte negar, seguendo il dritto e 'l giusto
de le dimande lor; ma dolce sempre

in both granting and denying. Oh, that these eyes	concedendo e negando. Oh, se questi occhi,
may get to see what I hope for,	anzi ch'ombra mortal li acciechi o copra,
before the shadow of death blinds or covers them:	giungon mai a veder quel ch'io ne spero:
most pleasant times, joyous hours!	soavissimi tempi, ore felici!
And I, despite the heavy weight of years of illness,	Felicissima me, serbata ancora,
still happily keeping	col grave incarco d'anni egri e infermi
at my dear service and sweet tasks,	a servitù sì cara, a sì dolci opre,
seeing the most benign queen,	a veder benignissima reina,
a queen I love like my soul,	reina da me amata al par de l'alma,
turned from an unhappy prisoner	fatta di prigioniera e infelice
into a lady and a fortunate, great woman!	signora e donna fortunata e grande!
May the sun shine yet another time, another day,	Splenda ancor una volta, un giorno, il sole
on the happy fate that I just envisioned,	al fortunato ben, ch'or fingo e formo,
and then may death, either quickly or slowly,	e chiuda morte poi rapida o lenta
shut my eyes to eternal night;	i languidi occhi in sempiterna notte;
for this sleep will be sweet, and the coffin	ché soave fie 'l sonno e caro letto
and tomb a welcome bed.[120]	il feretro e 'l sepolcro.
CHORUS: Sweet fields of Scotland and dear shores[121]	CORO: Dolci campi di Scozia e piagge care

120 "Will be" ("fie") is a zeugma, because it refers to both "sweet" and the following nouns ("the coffin / and tomb a welcome bed").

121 After the Lady-in-Waiting, it is now the Chorus' turn to give in to the reverie of a happy return to Scotland.

of my beloved homeland,	de la mia patria amata,
with the pleasant omen and hope	col presagio soave e con la speme
of a knowing, wise soul	d'anima saggia, accorta,
who rarely lacks true foresight,	cui raro falle antivedenza vera,
I hope to see you as well!	anch'io vedervi spero!
I hope to see again the Clyde and Forth[122]	Spero veder ancor Cluda e Fortea
bring the clearest waters to the ocean	trar l'acque a l'oceàn più che mai chiare,
and mix the fine sands with gold.	e mescer d'oro le minute arene.
I will see the stony, hard Cheviot,[123]	Vedrò il sassoso e duro Cheviota
adorn its horrid top	a freddo Borea, quasi ad aura estiva
with obscure palms	di tepid'Austro o Noto,
and unusual olive trees	ornar l'orrida chioma
in the cold north wind, as if	di sconosciuta palma
a summery breeze of mild south winds.[124]	e d'insolita oliva.
Pearls will reappear	Torneranno le perle
in my squalid, neglected hair;	a le neglette mie squallide chiome,
and, changing garments,	e variando vesta,
I will be dressed in white,	or candido ornerammi,
then green, then yellow, then dark,	or verde, or giallo, or perso,
then purple.	or purpureo colore.
I will follow my beautiful queen	Seguirò vaga la reina mia
into holy temples, to misty altars	ai sacri tempi, ai vaporanti altari
with their familiar Arabian scent.[125]	di caro arabo odore.
And I will see people bowing and honouring me	E vedrò in ampia e frequentata via
in wide and crowded streets.	chi m'inchini e m'onori.
Admired, I will admire,	Mirerò rimirata;

122 Two Scottish rivers.

123 Scottish mountain.

124 In the original, "Austro o Noto," which are two names designating a warm wind of the Adriatic Sea.

125 Incense.

but the gazes will differ:
covetous for others, perchance,
but always simple for me.
I will weave a wreath to the sweet sound
of a loving voice,
which in singing will express its desires,
and its tender sighs, in its song,
will make me smile sweetly.
But let this be nothing: only allow me
to pour perfumed waters
from golden, gem-encrusted vases
onto the royal hands,
and bring food to my queen,
contained in shiny silver,
and cut for the royal table
the noblest parts
of various foods:
let her accept them and take them
kindly, gravely, and smiling,
from a revering hand.

QUEEN: Oh, what things you picture and desire!
Thus does a beggar rave in his sleep,
when his dreams have shown him
a table of gems and gold.
But let a soul afflicted
by real troubles
cheer up with shades
of delectable fictions.[126]
Hope away, imagine, my friend!

ma fie vario lo sguardo:
cupido in altri forse,
e 'n me semplice fie.
Tesserommi ghirlanda al dolce suono
di voce innammorata,
che cantando m'adombri i suoi desiri,
e a me fien dolce riso
misti fra 'l canto i languidi sospiri.
Ma ciò sia nulla, e sol mi si conceda
versar acque odorate
da vasi aurei gemmati
a le mani reali,
e 'l cibo trarre a la reina mia
chiuso in lucido argento,
e di varia vivanda
secar a regia mensa
le parti più soavi:
ella le accetti e prenda
dolce, grave e ridente,
da mano riverente.

REINA: Deh, quai cose ti fingi, e quali agogni!
Tal nel sonno vaneggia
mendico, a cui colma appresenti il sogno
mensa di gemme e d'oro.
Ma concedasi ad alma travagliata
da verissimi affanni
sollevarsi con l'ombre
di dilettosi inganni.
Spera pur, fingi, amica:

126 In Italian, the noun "inganni" is closer to "deceits."

If I can give you nothing else to thank you,
I will imagine what you imagine,
believe what you believe;
but in the real future,
may the only glory
be the Lord's, not mine.[127]

s'altro dar non ti posso in tua mercede.
fingerò quel che fingi,
crederò quel che credi;
ma nel vero avenire
solo la gloria sia
del mio Signor, non mia.

CHORUS: How happily does the disused smile,
which appeared
on your dear mouth
when you spoke such sweet words,
my soul touch!
And like a pilgrim who, seeing
the rainy clouds clear at dusk –
showing a light
that promises a beautiful dawn –
is encouraged to walk,
so I, upon seeing your serene smile,
among gloomy and nebulous worries,
tread less sadly the painful road
of harsh captivity,
for your smile uncovers
for me a dearly welcome image
of beloved liberty.[128]

CORO: Il disusato riso, che s'è aperto
ne la tua cara bocca
or, al formar di tai dolci parole,
quanto soavemente
a me l'anima ha tocca!
E quasi peregrin, che 'n su la sera
miri nembo piovoso diradarsi,
onde si scopre imagine di sole,
promettendosi bella e chiara aurora,
al camin si rincora;
tal io tra fosche e nubilose cure,
del tuo riso al sereno
premo men grave la penosa via
de l'aspra prigionia,
discoprendomi il riso
cara imagine e grata
di libertade amata.

QUEEN: Let us enjoy these imagined dreams.

REINA: Pasciamci pur d'imaginate larve!

LADY: Behold, here comes with long strides

CAMERIERA: Mira, di là sen torna a lunghi passi

---

127 This marks the ultimate end of earthly hope, which coincides with the embracing of her God-given mission.

128 The beautiful simile of the pilgrim (which will return later in Mary's words) revolves around the theme of liberty.

the servant who came to us not long ago.[129]
What can it be? What will he say? He already
brought us good tidings, and perhaps now
he's back with ever better ones. Fortune
usually doubles its effects, and rarely
stops at the first one, be it good or bad.

SERVANT: Queen, the captain sends me
to tell you that soon the earls will be here
who came to negotiate with you. I have left them
as they left their dwelling, and it will not be long
before they are here.

QUEEN: Gladly let them come;
I will go inside and wait for them.

SERVANT: The captain sends me
to tell you the opposite, as he thinks it best
that you go down to meet them, if you were
in the upper chambers.[130]

QUEEN: Let my fate
have this too: I thank God,
who likes to humble me. I will wait for them here,

il servo ch'a noi venne ha poco d'ora:
che sarà? Che dirà? Liete novelle
già ci ha portato, e or con altre forse
lietissime ritorna. La fortuna
suol raddoppiar gli effetti, e rare volte
si ferma nel primiero, o buono o reo.

SERVO: Reina, a te mi manda il capitano,
per dirti com'or qui saranno i conti
venuti a trattar teco. Io già gli lascio
usciti de l'albergo, e tardar poco
potranno a giunger qui.

REINA: Vengan felici;
me n'entro ad aspettarli.

SERVO: Anzi per altro
mi manda il capitan, a cui par bene
che tu scendessi ad incontrargli, s'eri
ne le stanze sovrane.

REINA: Si conceda
questo anco a la mia sorte, e grazie a Dio,
cui piace umiliarmi. Io qui li aspetto,

---

129 Reality finally shatters the glass walls of the reverie sequence.
130 Further humiliation is demanded of Mary: she will have to greet her visitors, rather than wait for them to come greet her as a queen would expect and deserve.

since I am here; and if they also request
respects from an imprisoned queen,
I will reverently walk towards them;
may the Lord accept this! But what do you think?
What do they bring? Have you heard anything else
besides what you told us?

SERVANT: Nothing at all; but their minds are surely
occupied by serious things. Their frequent
private conversations, their denying one thing
and affirming another, as I can tell by their
gestures and moves, are clear indications
of thoughts regarding unclear things,
both difficult and important.

QUEEN: Oh, but let these things also be fair!

LADY: Hardly
does the useful match the honest.[131]
And this keeps the mind hanging, which cares
for both things. Setting you free
is the right thing, but perhaps not a useful one

poiché qui sono; e se richieggon anco
onori da reina prigioniera,
riverente vêr lor moverò il passo:
accetti il Signor l'opra! Ma che stimi?
Che portan seco? Hai nulla udito poscia,
più di quel che dicesti?

SERVO: Nulla invero; ma gravi cose certo
rivolgon ne la mente. Il tornar spesso
a ragionar fra loro, e negar questo
e quell'altro affermar, come si scorge
dai cenni e movimenti, indizio chiaro
son di pensier ch'aggiri dubbie cose
e difficili e grandi.

REINA: Oh, sian pur anco giuste!

CAMERIERA: Duramente
si congiunge con l'utile l'onesto:
e ciò sospesa tien la mente, ch'abbia
risguardo a l'un e l'altro. Il liberarti
è giusta cosa, ma non util forse

131 The Lady-in-Waiting's sententiousness is a clear break from her past forceful hopefulness.

for an ambitious woman[132]
who longs for your kingdom.

al consiglio di donna ambiziosa,
avida del tuo regno.

QUEEN: And I resolve to hear them
as proposals: may God
help me answer them.

REINA: E, quai proposte
mi propongh'io d'udir, a la risposta
aiutimi il mio Dio.

CHORUS: May freedom
be your goal, my queen, and may your tongue,
like a taut bow, fire the arrows
of your words only with the aim
to go back to reign.[133]

CORO: Il liberarti
sia tuo fine, o reina, e la tua lingua,
quasi arco teso, scocchi le saette
de le parole tue solo nel segno
di ritornar al regno.

QUEEN: I long to go back, for it is fair;
so what I will be able to say without offending
the eternal Kingdom and the royal print
impressed in my blood,
I will say all of it, to satisfy you,
and what's right, and myself.

REINA: Di ritornarvi bramo, perché è giusto;
così quel che potrò dir senza offesa
del Regno eterno e de la regia stampa
impressa nel mio sangue,
tutto dirò, per sodisfar a voi,
e al giusto, e a me medesma.

SERVANT: I feel it is wise
to adapt to events and times.

SERVO: Sento ch'è saggia cosa
farsi conformi agli accidenti e ai tempi.

With either low or high sails
does the helmsman navigate the loud,
treacherous waves, as the wind dictates.

Con vela or bassa, or alta
varca il nocchier l'onde sonanti, infide,
come gli detta il vento:

---

132 It bears remarking how the Lady-in-Waiting refers to the English queen as an "ambitious woman," a sign that she does not consider her to be an anointed sovereign like her mistress. The "your kingdom" in the following line also points out that she is regarded as illegitimate.

133 The simile, comparing her tongue to a bow and her words to arrows, can also be taken as representative of this tragedy as a whole: rather than putting Mary back on the throne, however, speech will ultimately succeed in making her story immortal.

Any means to reach the harbour
is good and fair. Here come the earls:
those who are in the front and carry
a silver sceptre are ministers,
and represent royal authority.

CHORUS: In such fashion, from the high windows
of the golden palace,
I used to see other beloved ministers,
faithful to my queen, come
with large followings.

QUEEN: They come with royal pomp
to a wretched, poor woman!

LADY-IN-WAITING: In this they show
honour and reverence. A royal woman
deserves royal worship: they already
bring you the insignia of a queen.

QUEEN: I will stop here
and wait for them.

LADY: To me, it would be
best to slowly move
towards them. Majesty can still be maintained
while honouring others.[134]

purché si giunga in porto,
ogni arte è buona e dritta. Or ecco i conti;
quei che vengon davanti e argenteo scettro
han su le spalle son ministri loro
e segno dan d'autorità reale.

CORO: Tali d'alta fenestra
di dorato palagio
vedev'io già venir con lunga schiera
più diletti ministri e più fedeli
a la reina mia.

REINA: Con regio fasto
vengon a donna misera e mendica!

CAMERIERA: In ciò dimostran segno
d'onor e riverenza: a regia donna
regio culto conviensi, e di reina
già ti portan l'insegne.

REINA: Io qui mi fermo
ad aspettarli.

CAMERIERA: A mio parer, ben fôra
moversi lentamente
inverso lor. Può maestà serbarsi
ed onorare altrui.

134 The Lady-in-Waiting's shift to pragmatism is striking, given her previous tone.

QUEEN: Let us go, then.

REINA: Moviamci dunque.

EARL OF PEMBROKE: How you trick us, oh heavens,
how you crush these mortal things! In what state
do I see you again, oh woman! In what state
did I see you, years ago![135]

C. di PEMBROCIA: Come ci aggiri, o Ciel, come travolvi
queste cose mortali! In quale stato
ti riveggio or, o donna! In qual ti vidi
ha già molt'anni!

QUEEN: Let this be an example
to those who live and those who reign; and let them see
how slippery is the soil where man's foot
leaves its print.[136] The life we lead
is a whirling wheel, where we are turned
by a hand now good, now bad; now high, now low.[137]

REINA: E questo esempio sia
a chi vive, a chi regna; e miri quanto
sia sdrucciolo il terreno, ove s'imprime
l'orma del piede umano: è mobil cerchio
la vita che corriamo, ove ci aggira
mano or placida or dura, or alto or basso.

EARL OF PEMBROKE: From what you say, I see such an image
that even what is living could not make more alive.

C. di PEMBROCIA: Di quel che dici, tal imagin veggio,
che non più vivo può mostrarsi il vivo.

QUEEN: Thanks go to whoever does it; forgiveness to whoever
is guilty and to whoever supports what's evil.

REINA: Grazie a chi 'l fa; perdono a chi n'ha colpa
e a chi 'l mal supporta.

EARL OF PEMBROKE: Speak only

C. di PEMBROCIA: Per te sola

135 Even the Earl of Pembroke struggles to come to terms with the deep personal transformation endured by the Queen. See Sanguineti White, *Dal detto alla figura*, 24.

136 She goes back to her very first lines in the tragedy, which already pointed to her life as an exemplar for other people, of both royal and lower birth.

137 The wheel of fortune image is back for one last time.

for yourself, for you alone support what's evil
and you alone are guilty.

QUEEN: Oh, let it be so!
May the error be not of two people, and
the punishment be of one. But the fault is divided,
and she who should have the least, bears the larger part!
I made mistakes, I confess, and thousands
of faults weigh down on my soul; but she who convicts me
is perhaps not innocent.[138]

EARL OF PEMBROKE: She is just and pious![139]

QUEEN: You can see it in me: I am witness,
judge, and culprit!

EARL OF PEMBROKE: I am sorry
to say you are also convicted.

QUEEN: I have been for many years: sadly, I feel it.

EARL OF PEMBROKE: If the fault grows, so may the punishment.

QUEEN: The sentence is just: I accept it.

parli, poiché tu sola il mal supporti
e sola n'hai la colpa.

REINA: Oh, così sia;
non sia di duo l'error, e sia la pena
di sol una. Ma 'l fallo si divide
e n'ha parte maggior chi men devria!
Errai, confesso, e mille colpe e mille
aggravan l'alma, ma chi me condanna,
non è innocente forse.

C. di PEMBROCIA: È giusta e pia!

REINA: In me si vede: io testimonio sono
e son giudice e reo!

C. di PEMBROCIA: Così mi pesa
dirti ch'anco sei tu la condennata.

REINA: Già di molt'anni 'l son: purtroppo il sento.

C. di PEMBROCIA: Dove cresce l'error, cresca la pena.

REINA: È giusta la sentenza, io la confermo.

138 Although she has already accepted the inevitability of her fate, Mary is determined to let her reasons be heard by her rival's emissaries.

139 The following exchange is in the form of a stichomythia (one- or two-line alternating speeches), which speeds up the rhythm and denotes an animated dispute.

EARL OF PEMBROKE: An obstinate fault is double, and weighs as much.	C. di PEMBROCIA: Fallo ostinato è doppio, e doppio aggrava.
QUEEN: And increases as much as obstinacy grows old.	REINA: E cresce quanto ostinazion s'invecchia.
EARL OF PEMBROKE: So it increased in you, oh woman,[140] for whom many heavy years and a long captivity have not changed or bent the hardened mind; rather, more obstinately you deny, when you should yield.	C. di PEMBROCIA: Così in te crebbe, o donna, a cui molt'anni durissimi a portarsi e prigion lunga non han potuto l'indurata mente o smover o piegar; anzi ostinata più neghi, allorché più conceder déi.
QUEEN: I deny nothing that a pious and just mind could consent to.	REINA: Nulla nego io, che consentir si possa da mente giusta e pia.
EARL OF PEMBROKE: But you contradict the royal demand of a noble queen, who is not to be denied not only of what she asks, but of what she hints or thinks.	C. di PEMBROCIA: Ma contradici a dimanda real d'alta reina, cui sconviensi negar, non quel che chiede, ma quel che accenna o pensa.
QUEEN: This law is to be observed and obeyed where the royal voice has rightful power.[141] Let those who were born kings command and only be subjected to laws and right.[142]	REINA: Ove la real voce ha giusto impero questa legge s'osservi e s'ubidisca. Chi nacque re commandi e sol soggiaccia a le leggi e al dritto.

140 He denies her the title of queen.

141 Divine right.

142 As she did in her real life, the fictional Mary refuses Elizabeth's authority to try or sentence her.

EARL OF PEMBROKE: Those who are at another's mercy and who can only do with themselves what others want, I call servants.	C. di PEMBROCIA: Io servo chiamo chi è in altrui poter e di se stesso sol può quel ch'altri vuole.
QUEEN: Rather, servants are those who want what they must not. A tormented soul is chained and enslaved, while the crown sits on the head of an unlawful king: a noose around the neck, chains around the feet.	REINA: Anzi, chi vuole quel che non deve è servo: anima torta è catenata e schiava. E la corona porta re ingiusto in capo; al collo, ai piedi ha catena, ha capestro.
EARL OF PEMBROKE: Yet he has the power to acquit and punish as he likes.[143]	C. di PEMBROCIA: E pur ha forza d'assolvere e punir com'a lui pare.
QUEEN: Such is even the power of a bandit in the woods, who, armed, can take mantle and life from a king, if he falls into his clutches unarmed.	REINA: Tal ha forza anco masnadiero in selva, che puote armato tôrre e manto e vita al maggior re, se disarmato e solo ne le sue insidie cade.
EARL OF PEMBROKE: But do not call unjust he who acts upon the advice of just men before he pronounces his judgment.	C. di PEMBROCIA: Ma non si chiami ingiusto chi 'l consiglio d'uomini giusti adopra, anzi che scioglia al giudizio la voce.
QUEEN: I do not call him that.	REINA: Io tal nol chiamo.

143 The use of masculine nouns and pronouns is deliberate: Mary talks about a king, not a queen, and the Earl of Pembroke continues in this fashion.

EARL OF PEMBROKE: You will therefore not call my queen unjust.[144]	C. di PEMBROCIA: Non chiamerai dunque la mia reina ingiusta.
QUEEN: I will say nothing: let this prison, where I am trapped, answer for me.	REINA: Io nulla dico, ma risponda per me questa prigione ove son chiusa.
EARL OF PEMBROKE: And to keep its answer short we come to take you away from it.	C. di PEMBROCIA: E perché non risponda lungamente noi ten veniamo a sciôr.
QUEEN: It is high time: thank you for coming here, oh just ministers, to carry out such just work![145]	REINA: N'è tempo omai, e grazie a voi, che qui giusti venite ministri a sì giust'opra!
EARL OF PEMBROKE: Here is proof of the authority that we were bestowed to execute what I say. This is the royal seal, and do you recognize these notes? They are the queen's, written in her own hand.	C. di PEMBROCIA: Ecco la fede di quella autorità ch'a noi è data di poter essequir quanto ti dico. Questo è regio sigillo e queste note, le riconosci, son de la reina, formate di sua mano.
QUEEN: I recognize both: I have seen them many times.	REINA: E l'uno e l'altro riconosco: già molte n'ho veduto.
EARL OF PEMBROKE: Now unfold them and read.	C. di PEMBROCIA: Or spiega tutto e leggi.
CHORUS: Oh, beloved paper, which brings us freedom! … But the queen	CORO: O cara carta che libertà ci apporti!... Ma si turba

144 The masculine, confined to the hypothetical, is abandoned, and the feminine is brought back to talk about the real circumstances.

145 Mary's exaggerated enthusiasm is not devoid of bitter sarcasm in light of what is about to unfold.

frowns in reading and grows pale.	la reina leggendo e impallidisce...
QUEEN: Disused happiness unsettles like pain does. But hush, so I can read all of it. The beginning is sweet and lovely: if the middle and end are such, we shall soon be free.	REINA: Disusata allegrezza turba come dolore. Ma tacete, infin ch'io tutto legga: è caro e dolce il principio, e se tal è 'l mezzo e 'l fine, libere sarem tosto.
LADY-IN-WAITING: Oh heavens, oh God, thank you for so much mercy!	CAMERIERA: O Cielo, o Dio, grazie di grazia tanta!
EARL OF CUMBERLAND: Rather, let me spare you the trouble which you may feel in reading: hear this. In short: the path to your freedom is a hard one, but still useful and straight: "Let this head be detached from the neck, and let the soul fly where it must, and go freely: this is allowed to it."[146]	C. di COMBERLANDA: Anzi, perché si tolga a te la noia, che leggendo aver puoi, senti e ascolta in brevissime note la via di liberarti: è dura via, ma pur utile e dritta. — Si discioglia dal collo quella testa, e l'alma voli poi dove deve, e 'n libertà sen vada, ché ciò le si concede. —
QUEEN: From such a hand, I was expecting such a blow. Take your papers: an unfaithful mind	REINA: Da tal mano tal colpo s'aspettava. Togli le carte tue: mente infedele

146 Elizabeth's ultimate mockery: after so long tolerating Mary's defiance of her authority, she seizes the opportunity to take a final jab at her rival (employing, moreover, religious imagery).

wrote them; no longer will they be in a faithful hand.[147]

CHORUS: Oh, what do I see!

QUEEN: She who sends you here and wrote this
seems to be yearning and hungry
for human blood:
the pious blood of the many she murdered
(with what right, may God judge in heaven!)
is not enough for her greedy thirst,[148]
so much that she also calls me to blood,
to me, whose blood I am
of the blood whence she was born![149]

CHORUS: Oh, terrible words!
What blood does she speak of?

QUEEN: What did I do? What did I say,
for the road to open
to such cruelty?

EARL OF CUMBERLAND: Now is not the time
to blame others or be sorry.

QUEEN: It is time to die, I see that!

le scrisse; non più stian in man fedele!

CORO: Ohimé, ohimé, che veggio!

REINA: Ben par che vaga e ingorda
è de l'umano sangue
chi te manda e qui scrive,
poiché non basta a l'avida sua sete
il sangue pio di tanti e tanti occisi,
(con qual giustizia, in ciel giudichi Dio!)
ché 'l sangue anco a me chiama,
a me, che sangue sono
del sangue ond'ella nacque!

CORO: Ahi, dura voce!
Di che sangue si parla?

REINA: Che fec'io, che diss'io,
perché s'aprisse il varco
a tanta crudeltade?

C. di COMBERLANDA: Altro conviensi
or, ch'incolpar altrui o che dolersi.

REINA: Morir conviene, il veggio!

147 "Faithful" and "unfaithful" are ambiguous adjectives, referring to both human trust (and lack thereof) and to religious observance (and lack thereof).
148 The monstrous portrayal of Elizabeth continues.
149 The theme of family ties comes back in this moment of utter distress.

But at least let me say
that she who kills me
is impious in killing me.

Ma non si torrà almeno
il dir che chi m'occide
empiamente m'occide.

CHORUS: Alas, what words
do I hear, my queen!
Who will die? Who will kill?

CORO: Misera, quai parole
sento! O reina mia,
chi morirà, chi occide?

QUEEN: I, I will be killed,
my daughters! And the killer
of your queen
is the cruel woman
whose rightful heiress I am![150]

REINA: Io, io sarò l'occisa,
o figlie! E micidiale
de la vostra reina
è la donna crudele,
di cui son giusta erede!

LADY-IN-WAITING: You, killed? My mistress,
you, my queen and life?
You, killed? Alas, what do you say?

CAMERIERA: Occisa te, mia donna,
te, mia reina e vita?
occisa te? Misera me, che dici?

QUEEN: This head[151] is demanded,
and where gold necklaces once lay,
there the sharp blade[152] will cut.
Such is the road
to my freedom!

REINA: Questa testa si chiede,
e dove già mi cinse aureo monile
passerà il ferro acuto.
Tale strada s'insegna
a la mia libertade!

CHORUS: Let it pierce my heart, my throat,
and may my head be severed
from my neck, as a gift
to she who demands your head!

CORO: Passi per questo cor, per questa gola,
e dal collo disciolta
sia la mia testa, dono
di chi testa dimanda!

---

150 The fact that Mary self-identifies as Elizabeth's rightful heiress brings again the spotlight on the kinship between the two women: in this articulation, Elizabeth is portrayed as a cruel mother.

151 The head, as Sanguineti White remarks, is both a political and human symbol (*Dal detto alla figura*, 35–7).

152 The "gold necklace" ("aureo monile") of the previous line is a stark contrast to the "sharp blade" ("ferro acuto"). Della Valle opts for the synecdoche "ferro" (iron), indicating the blade's material.

EARL OF CUMBERLAND: The punishment must go whence the guilt came.	C. di COMBERLANDA: Vada la pena onde la colpa venne.
QUEEN: The guilt came from me: my guilt was to believe too much someone I shouldn't have! And yet belief was expected from woman to woman, from queen to queen, from niece to aunt.[153]	REINA: Da me la colpa venne; colpa di creder troppo a chi meno devea! Ma pur creder devea donna a donna, e reina a reina, a la zia la nipote.
EARL OF CUMBERLAND: Words are in vain where necessity forces one to act:[154] the time you spend lamenting and blaming others you should invest in something more useful. Think of what you need for your next life: little is left for you of this one.	C. di COMBERLANDA: Vane son le parole, ove necessità costringe a l'opra: l'ora, che lamentando spendi e incolpando altrui, in ufficio più utile consuma. Pensa a quel che conviene per l'altra vita; ché di questa breve poco spazio t'avanza.
QUEEN: Compassionate advice from a cruel adviser! But is so little time left to my wretched life that I have no time to cry for my death as I wish to?	REINA: O consiglio pietoso di consiglier crudele! Ma sì poc'ora resta a la misera vita, ch'anco non abbia tempo a voglia mia di pianger la mia morte?
EARL OF CUMBERLAND: The sun that you now see fall down into the sea will be the last one that your eyes will behold.	C. di COMBERLANDA: Questo sol, che tu miri precipitando già cader nel mare, sarà l'ultimo sole che veggian gli occhi tuoi.

153 The already exploited subject of kinship and female ties resurfaces powerfully.

154 A Machiavellian postulation in the context of an exaggeratedly mean-spirited speech by the Earl of Cumberland.

CHORUS: Oh, injuring cruelty,
the cruelty of a tiger,
for whom harming,
and harming and killing are one instant,
one instant which fuses
death and life![155]

QUEEN: For a long time I have seen
the sharp tip of such an unjust blade
dangle over my head.
And like a pilgrim[156] who at the break of dawn
decides to leave his nightly shelter,
adapts to the darkness and covers
his painful feet, and on his hunched
shoulders places the small bundle where
his belongings are stored, takes his
trusted cane, and only waits
for the east to grow brighter; so I,
in the bitterest, most shameful night
of my misfortunes, waiting only

CORO: O fiera crudeltade,
o crudeltà di tigre,
cui giungere a ferire
e ferir e occidere è un sol punto,
e 'n un punto confonde
con la vita la morte!

REINA: Già lungo spazio, veggio
pender sul capo mio l'acuta punta
di così ingiusto ferro.
E quasi peregrin, ch'al far de l'alba
si consigli lasciar notturno albergo,
fra le tenebre ancor s'adatta e veste
il duro piede e a l'incurve spalle
impone il picciol fascio, ove ravolte
porta le sue fortune, indi, ripresa
la sua compagna verga, solo attende
che s'apra l'oriente; tale anch'io
ne la notte acerbissima e indegna
de le sventure mie, solo aspettando

155 Now Elizabeth is dehumanized by being compared to a tiger. The animal imagery of the tiger (previously anticipated by the lion metaphor, v. 1057) is ideally suited to Mary's status as a sacrificial victim.

156 The pilgrim simile, which had already been used by the Chorus as a symbol of hope, comes back in the Queen's speech to indicate the opposite. This time, the second object of the simile is her, walking towards the executioner's sharp blade, her fate determined by God's invisible hand.

for the final moment of my final walk,	al mio estremo camin l'ora prescritta,
with my soul clad in suffering,	di sofferenza l'anima vestita,
and with the bundle of my grave errors placed	e posto il fascio dei miei gravi errori
on the same humeri of He who wanted	sovra gli omeri amici di Chi volse
to bear it Himself, with the strong	sopra sé tôrlo, con la verga forte
cane of hope, born in the middle of a sea	de la speranza nata in mezzo al mare
of infinite piety, I have readied	d'infinita pietade, apparecchiato
my foot to the difficult path that you assign to me.	ho 'l piede al duro passo che m'ascrivi.
But since the crossing is too terrible and obscure,	Ma perché orrido è troppo e dubbio 'l varco
and those who feel most confident fail the most,	e più falle chi più vi si assicura,
I need more time before my journey.	qualche spazio maggior chiamo al viaggio.
Extend not my life, but rather extend	Non s'allunghi la vita, ma s'allunghi
my time to think of how I lived	il tempo di pensar come son vissa
and how I must die.	o come ho da morire.
I ask for a minor favour, which takes nothing	Lieve grazia dimando, e nulla toglie
from her who can give it to me. Let these eyes weep	a chi darla mi può: piangan questi occhi
for my faults for one more day,	un altro sole ancor le colpe mie,
and then let my wretched head, which you ask of me,	e la testa infelice, che mi chiami,
be at the mercy of the mercy that I ask.	sia poi mercé de la mercé ch'io chiamo.
EARL OF CUMBERLAND: You were given much time, and much risk	C. di COMBERLANDA: Lungo spazio s'è dato e lungo rischio
did a head worthier than yours endure.	ha corso testa de la tua più degna:
May shame be removed from the face	tolgasi omai del volto la vergogna
of my noble queen	de l'alta mia reina,
that a captive woman,	che donna prigioniera

and wretched, and beggarly,	e misera e mendica
dared to plot against her	ardisca contra lei di tesser frodi
and endanger her life.	e perigli di vita.
QUEEN: How true it is	REINA: Ahi, com'è vero
that an unjust heart brings confidence to itself	che cor ingiusto, in oltraggiando altrui,
by insulting others! Her own faults,	a sé sicurtà toglie! Il proprio fallo,
believe me, make your queen fear,	credimi, fa temer la tua reina,
not my deceits or tricks.	non arte o insidia mia.
EARL OF CUMBERLAND: You still dare	C. di COMBERLANDA: Ancor ardisci
to lay the blame where honour is due?	di gettar biasmi, ove tu devi onori?
Go back in there at once, and soon you shall see	Vanne tosto là entro, e vedrai tosto
whether the error is another's or yours!	se 'l fallo è altrui o tuo!
CHORUS: Oh, sinful hand,	CORO: Ahi, empia mano,
thus you do push and press	così sospingi e premi
a royal body? And yet you live? Let us help her,	real persona, e vivi? Soccorriamla,
let us avenge her, sisters, or let us die with her!	vendichiamla, sorelle, o moriam seco!
QUEEN: My friends, help	REINA: Amiche mie, il soccorso
and revenge will be to beg forgiveness	e la vendetta sia pregar perdono
for him, who now offended me,	a lui, ch'ora m'offende,
and for me, who am offended.	e a me, che son offesa.
May your heart quiet down: and if it	Quetisi 'l vostro cor; e se 'l mi deste
was once obedient to me,	un tempo ubidiente,
now may it be calm and pained,	datelmi or, vi prego,
I beg of you.	placido e sofferente.
I go to die, I go to end	Io me ne vo a morir, io vo a finire
my harsh misery.	l'aspra miseria mia;
I go happy and content,	men vo contenta e lieta,

except for leaving you	se non quanto vi lascio
as abandoned virgins, and in whose hands	vergini abbandonate, e in man a cui
I do not know, nor do I know what will become of you,	no 'l so, né so che fie poscia di voi,
after I have left you.[157]	poi che v'avrò lasciate.
May that God who accepts everyone accept you;	Accettivi quel Dio che tutti accetta:
may He be your guide and shield.	Ei vi sia guida e schermo:
This I humbly and warmly pray of Him,	di ciò umilmente e caldamente il prego,
among my final prayers.	fra le preghiere estreme.
LADY-IN-WAITING: Where are you going, queen?	CAMERIERA: Ove ne vai, reina?
Where, my life? Where are you leaving me?	Ove ne vai, mia vita? Ove mi lasci?
I, who was always by your side	Me, che sempre fui teco
throughout your life,	nel corso de la vita,
now you leave me without you	dunque or senza te lasci
when death has come?	nel passo de la morte?
You grew up in these arms, in these arms	Crescesti in queste braccia, in queste braccia
you will die, if die you must.[158]	morrai, s'hai da morire;
Nothing will take you from here, if not that blade:	né di qui ti trarrà se non il ferro.
the cruel blade that is	Il ferro, che crudele
ready for your demise.	s'apparecchia al tuo danno,
Alas, alas,	ohimé, ohimé,
may that weapon strike me and sever me	quel ferro me trafigga e me recida
in thousands of thousands of gashes,	in mille squarci e mille,
before I be separated from you!	pria che da te mi svella!

157 In this moment, as indeed throughout the tragedy, Della Valle emphasizes the coexistence, in Mary's person, of a human and a divine nature. Rather than embracing the almost frenzied longing for martyrdom of early Christian martyrs, this modern woman cannot forget her earthly attachments, and the people that have accompanied her along her path.

158 Now it is the Lady-in-Waiting, and not the Queen, who speaks like a mother. As such, Mary will address her in her following speech.

QUEEN: Mother, you long showed me
that you love me, and I always kept my faith in it.
And your love was once
dear and helpful to me:
now it is dear and harmful, for I see
that I have to thank you for it
with tears and pain.
Forgive me, and take
what it gives me to give you
the saddest fate.
Let not my pain grow greater:
let not my eyes see, in their final glimpses,
such a sorry sight
that you, forcefully taken
from the body you now embrace and hold in vain,
should fall to the ground, and that your white,
revered hair should spread
across your venerable face.
You did much, loved
much, and served:
now let me go
where my God commands,
and only place your dear cheek
near my cheek.
Take this as a sign
that I appreciate your will:
let this be the final gift,
to you from a friend,
to me from a sister.[159]

REINA: Madre, assai lungamente m'hai mostrato
che tu m'ami, e tal fede io n'ebbi sempre;
e m'è stato il tuo amore
caro e utile un tempo:
or m'è caro e dannoso, poiché veggio
ch'ho da darten mercede
di pianto e di dolore.
Perdonami, e ricevi
quel che mi dà per darti
miserissima sorte.
Non m'accrescer più male;
non veggian gli occhi miei nei guardi estremi
sì dolorosa vista,
che tu divelta a forza
dal corpo, ch'or abbracci e 'n vano stringi,
caggia a terra, e la chioma
canuta e riverenda si disperga
sul venerabil volto!
Assai hai fatto, assai
hai amato, hai servito:
lasciami ch'io men vada
ove 'l mio Dio commanda,
e solo aggiungi a questa guancia mia
la cara guancia tua.
Ciò ricevi per segno
ch'io gradisco il volere:
questo sia 'l dono estremo
a te d'una tua amica,
a me d'una sorella.

159 In these touching lines, the ever-present theme of female ties takes centre stage, this time in a positive, virtuous way, as opposed to its evil counterpart in reference to Elizabeth.

LADY-IN-WAITING: This I shall give you at once,
but then I will die with you, my queen.
This is what I want: if you don't, forgive me!
Oh, cheek! Oh, dear cheek!
How happily I loved you,
how faithfully I embellished you,
how sadly now I kiss you! Alas!

CAMERIERA: Ciò ti darò ben tosto,
ma morrò poscia teco, o mia reina:
così vogl'io! Se tu no 'l vuoi, perdona.
Ahi guancia! Ahi guancia cara!
Quanto lieta t'amai,
quanto fedel t'ornai,
quanto mesta or ti bacio! Ahi, ahi, ahimé!

QUEEN: Now leave me and follow me, if you are
allowed to by those who hold power over us.
Follow me to bitter death,
and help me with prayer.
There is nothing you can give me
that would be more useful and beneficial. Oh heaven, oh sun,
I will never see you again
from this unhappy prison!

REINA: Or mi lascia e mi segui, se seguirmi
ti concede chi forza ha sovra noi.
Seguimi al duro passo
e con prieghi m'aita.
Nulla più puoi tu darmi
che più mi vaglia o giovi. O cielo, o sole,
non vi vedrò più mai
da prigion infelice!

LADY-IN-WAITING: I will follow you, my queen:
what else could I do that would please me more?
These feet will follow your steps
until death, and then
your soul will follow my soul,
unbound from this flesh.[160]

CAMERIERA: Seguirò, mia reina;
e che poss'io più far, che più mi piaccia?
Seguiran questi piedi i passi tuoi
sin a la morte, e poi
seguirà l'alma tua l'anima mia,
sciolta da queste carni.

CHORUS: Will we not follow?
Will we remain alive,
if our heart dies,
if our queen dies?
Let us go, let us die with her!

CORO: E noi non seguiremo?
Rimarrem vive noi,
se muor il nostro core,
se muor la mia reina?
Andiam, moriam con lei!

160 The image of the soul freed from the flesh had already been presented by the Queen, with the same lexical choices, when theorizing the immortality of her body politic (vv. 926–7).

EARL OF CUMBERLAND: Stop these women! And you, soldier,
don't let them in.

C. di COMBERLANDA: Ferminsi queste donne! E tu, soldato,
vieta loro l'entrata.

QUEEN: Oh, daughters, farewell,
I shall see you elsewhere,
in a freer, more serene chamber:
until we see one another in heaven!

REINA: O figlie, a Dio,
a rivederci altrove,
in più libera stanza e più serena,
a rivederci in Cielo!

CHORUS: Cruel man! Why do you forbid us
to see the woman die who kept us alive
while she was alive?
Let us instead die with her!

CORO: Crudel, perché ci togli
poter veder morire,
anzi morir con chi ci tenne in vita,
mentre ci restò vita?

BUTLER: My Lord,[161] I know you reign and live up above,
and are wherever life is.
This I believe, and it is true
that, just and pious,
you rule over human things and throw
spears of reward and punishment for our actions.
Yet, I often saw
the oppressed innocent
fall, and their lot
so lowly and vile, as low as the soil
and almost like mud, be trodden upon and crushed.
And on the other side, the haughty head
rises and merges with clouds
and wants, and demands, and obtains,

MAGGIORDUOMO: Signor, io so che là su regni e vivi,
e sei dovunque è vita.
Questo credo, ed è vero
che giusto insieme e pio
volvi le cose umane, e premi e pene
libri con lance a le nostr'opre eguale.
E pur vidi sovente
oppresso l'innocente
cader, e la sua sorte
sì bassa e vil, che, col terren congiunta,
pur quasi fango si calpesta e preme.
E d'altra parte sorge,
e con le nubi mesce
l'altiera testa, e vuole, e chiama, e impetra,

161 The Butler launches a tirade against God's confounding ways, echoing that of Job in the Old Testament.

and speaks, and commands, and rules over right and wrong
with a firm and proud hand,[162]
over what is unjust and impious, and disposes of other people's
wills and lives by her own will.
What can I say, if not that your judgment
and laws, with which you govern our actions,
are tall abysses,[163]
whose sacred depths
our virtue cannot reach,
falling down senseless if it tries?
Mary of Scotland dies, and Elizabeth
of England kills her![164]

CHORUS: Alas, what do I hear!
My lady has died,
my life has died![165]

BUTLER: She lives still, sisters,
the wretched queen
of most wretched, miserable people.
She lives, but only the end
of her life is left to her.
Rather, only the pains and woes
of which life is full are left to her.

e dice, e impera, e volge il dritto e 'l torto
con man superba e forte,
l'ingiusto e l'empio; e come di sua voglia
fa de la vita e de la voglia altrui.
Che poss'io dir, se non che i tuoi giudìci
e le leggi, con cui l'opre governi,
sono altissimi abissi,
al cui sacro profondo
virtù nostra non giunge,
e stolta cade, se poggiarvi tenta?
Muore Maria di Scozia e Isabella
d'Inghilterra l'occide!

CORO: Ohimé, che sento!
È morta la mia donna,
è morta la mia vita!

MAGGIORDUOMO: Vive ancor, o sorelle,
la misera reina
di genti miserissime e meschine:
vive, ma de la vita
solo le resta il fine.
Anzi le restan solo i danni e i mali,
di che piena è la vita.

162 On the depersonalization of Elizabeth through synecdoche ("head") and the function of the use of polysyndeton, see Introduction, p. 18.

163 The inscrutability of God's law is emphasized by this powerful oxymoron.

164 The Queen of Scots is named for the first time in the tragedy, together with Elizabeth: yet again, the two women are halves of the same whole.

165 The Chorus misunderstands the Butler's emotional words, taking them for a factual communication, rather than a projection of what is bound to happen. It is nonetheless meaningful that the actual death of the Queen will later be pronounced by the Chorus itself, who had felt it in its soul (v. 1977).

CHORUS: She has been on this harsh journey
on such a harsh mission,
for many years now!
But what do they say? What are they doing in there?

CORO: Già molt'anni corr'ella
in sì duro viaggio,
sotto sì duro incarco!
Ma che dicon? Che fanno colà entro?

BUTLER: What do I know? All is bad,
all is tears and sorrow,
all is contempt and scorn.

MAGGIORDUOMO: Che so io? Tutto è male,
tutto è lagrime e doglia,
tutto è disprezzo e scherno.

CHORUS: Oh, impious, cruel people!
Oh, heinous minds!

CORO: Ahi, empie e crude genti!
ahi, scelerate menti!

BUTLER: They left her little time to live.[166]
And, since she was followed inside
by that evil crowd, once she came
to the innermost chamber she looked
calmly and humbly at those who
were going after her, who have the greatest
authority in this business, and said: "Here,
friends, let your following me
come to an end, I beg you,
and leave me alone
with this little life I am left.
Prepare
what is needed for my death,

MAGGIORDUOMO: Dato le han poco spazio ancor di vita:
ed ella, poiché dentro
venne seguita da la cruda schiera,
che qui veduto avrete, essendo giunta
a la più interna stanza, rivolgendo
gli occhi placida e umìle a quei che seco
venian a par, ch'autorità maggiore
hanno in quest'opra, ha detto: — Qui finisca,
amici, prego, il vostro venir meco,
e lasciate me sola
questo poco di vita che m'è data.
Apparecchiate voi
quel che conviensi per la morte mia,

166 The Butler, who was an eyewitness to various stages of the Queen's life, will serve as the chronicler of her last moments, including her execution. In this way, as will be evident later, the gory components of the beheading can be kept offstage and only presented via narrative, in accordance with classical tradition.

and I will prepare	ch'io farò l'apparecchio
for my next life. Grant	per l'altra vita. Ciò dato mi sia
this to me, if you please, out of mercy	per grazia, se volete,
or human compassion."	o per pietade umana. —
"This," one of them said, "will be granted you;	— Ciò — detto ha l'un di lor — dato ti sia;
but you have little time	ma sia breve lo spazio
for what you ask." She, with sad	a l'opera che chiedi. — Ella con gli occhi
and tranquil eyes, consented,	gravi e tranquilli ha consentito e, dentro
entered inside, and pulled the door behind her,	entrata, spinto ha l'uscio per serrarsi,
but she was pushed aside, and thus quietly	ma n'è stata sospinta; e quindi queta
she went inside, and with her face	ritiratasi a dentro, il volto tinto
tainted by sorrow and pity	di dolor e pietade,
looked at me, who was near her.	me, che l'era vicino, ha rimirato.
My eyes were full	Avev'io gli occhi pregni
of tears for that painful sight,	de le lacrime sorte a l'aspra vista,
for that miserable spectacle; but then	al misero spettacolo; ma scorse
they started running down my cheeks	son allor per le guance
so thickly that she, noticing	con così larga riga, ch'ella, accorta
my crying, said serenely: "What is happening?	del mio pianto, serena, ha detto: — Che hai?
Are you crying for my life	Piangi tu la mia vita
or my freedom?"[167]	o la mia libertade? —
CHORUS: Alas, for such life	CORO: Ohimé, ché vita tale
and such freedom	e cotal libertade
are my prison and death![168]	è mia prigione e morte!
BUTLER: "I cry …" I said,	MAGGIORDUOMO: — I' piango — ho detto,

167 These words are spoken in true martyr-like fashion.

168 The chiasmus is distributed over three lines ("life / […] freedom / […] prison and death").

and wanted to say more, but pain cut off
my words and voice.
"Pray for me, my friend,"
she then added,
"this is a more pious action
and more beneficial."
She could not utter these words
without her eyes getting red and unveiling
fresh tears.
Thence, she left me and, turning her eyes
to the cross hung above her bed,
she walked towards it with open arms[169]
and, once she reached it, she kissed it ardently,
touching her mouth to its feet, where she lingered
for a long time. And then she let herself go,
falling to her knees, with her eyes fixed
upon it, and loudly she sobbed
and sighed, and then she bowed her head,
so much that it almost touched the ground.
She beat her chest with her right hand with all her strength,
repeatedly, and did so again and again,
sighing and weeping.

CHORUS: May these sighs appease your wrath,
my Lord, and take them

e altro volea dir; ma 'l duol m'ha tronca
la parola e la voce.
— Prega per me, amico,
ha soggiunt'ella allora,
quest'è ufficio più pio
ed è d'util maggiore. —
Non ha potuto dir queste parole
senza rossor negli occhi, e la nascente
lacrima s'è scoperta.
Quinci, lasciato me, volgendo il guardo
a la croce, ch'è appesa a capo al letto,
vêr lei s'è mossa con le braccia aperte
e al giunger le ha dato un bacio ardente,
figgendo al piè la bocca, ove gran pezza
s'è ferma. E poi, se stessa abbandonando,
caduta ginocchion, con gli occhi fissi
in lei, alti singulti, alti sospiri
ha dato, e quinci declinando il capo,
sì che quasi a toccar giungea la terra,
a più poter con la man destra il petto
s'è percosso più volte e ripercosso,
sospirando e gemendo.

CORO: Plachino l'ira tua questi sospiri,
Signor, e li ricevi

169 The open arms are a Christological symbol; see Introduction, p. 18.

as the price of pity!

BUTLER: At last, wanting to
stand up but hindered by the pain
and weakness that long afflicted her,[170]
she fell on her left hand,
and down to the ground,
and in falling tipped over. In seeing that,
I ran to help her, and the Earl of Pembroke
followed me, he held her
under one arm and I under the other,
and as we lifted her, she turned to us
and peacefully said: "Pain and age
give you this weight, the heavy weight
of a useless woman. May God give you merit
for this last action for my benefit!"
Once she stood up, she kissed the cross, and with reverence
removed it from the nail whence it hung,
and, holding it to her chest:
"My friends," she said, "let us go, here is my guide,
here is the food and relief
to what little journey I am left,

per prezzo di pietade!

MAGGIORDUOMO: Alfin, volendo
levarsi, grave dal dolor e forse
da quella debiltà, che già contratta
ha lungamente, è ricaduta sopra
la man sinistra, e con lei dato ha in terra,
e 'n cader s'è rivolta. Io, ciò veggendo,
son corso ad aiutarla, e me seguito
ha 'l conte di Pembrocia, il qual l'ha presa
sotto l'un de le braccia, io sotto l'altro,
e 'n sollevarla, a noi volgendo il volto,
placidissima ha detto: — Il mal e gli anni
vi dànno or questo peso, peso grave
d'inutil donna. Iddio merto vi dia
di quest'ultimo ufficio in util mio! —
Sorta, bacia la croce e riverente
dal chiodo la discioglie, ove pendea,
e strettalasi al petto:
— Amici, andiamo: — dice — ecco la guida,
ecco 'l cibo e 'l ristoro
a quel poco viaggio, che mi resta,

170 The reference is both to an exaggerated old age, and to the sciatica that, according to a number of reports, afflicted her. Her difficulty walking, which will come back later, is also noted in Sartorio Loschi's *Letter* (Appendix).

and I am ready for it. But if a miserable	a cui son pronta. Ma se puote ancora
sinner is still graced	misera peccatrice aver mercede
with a few hours to live, please grant	di poc’ore di vita, si conceda
a little more time to be spent	a questa che ’l vi chiede
in holy acts	qualche spazio maggiore, il qual si spenda
to this one who begs you. Let a king,	in ufficio pietoso. Un re, figliolo
the son of a wretched mother,	di madre sventurata,
receive from his mother, before she dies,	riceva da sua madre, anzi che mora,
if not her last kisses	se non gli estremi baci
and her last words,	e l’estreme parole,
at least her dying wishes.	almen gli avisi del camin estremo.
I need some time and ink	Spazio chiamo e inchiostro
to write a few notes,	a scriver poche note,
which you will see and read,	ch’esser potran da voi vedute e lette,
to be sent to my son.	per mandarle a mio figlio.
This is nothing for those who can give it,	Nulla è questo a chi dona,
but a lot for she who asks it.” The earls	a chi dimanda è molto. — In dubbio han posto
debated on her request; yet, at last,	i conti la richiesta; pur, al fine
they allowed her to write, and I’ve just left her	han permesso che scriva, e io la lascio
seated, writing.	or assisa scrivendo.
I left by force, for I was forced	La lascio a forza; poich’a forza m’hanno
out of there.	cacciato di là entro.
CHORUS: And where	CORO: E dove resta
is the trusty lady-in-waiting?	la fida cameriera?
BUTLER: The poor woman	MAGGIORDUOMO: La meschina
collapsed from heavy panting.	caduta è di dolore in grave ambascia.
Now she is on a bed, and her old servant	Or riman sovra un letto e a lei sopra

is crying next to her.	piange la vecchia serva.
But here come the earls,	Ma già di là discende la famiglia
and behind them are the executioners	dei conti, e dietro lor mira i ministri
with their silver maces.	con l'argentate mazze.
CHORUS: Oh, what a painful, horrid sight!	CORO: Ahi vista acerba e dura!
I tremble, tremble and behold,	Tremo, tremo, mirando,
and wait for what is to come. Alas!	aspettando che segue, ohimé, ohimé!
Behold my queen,	Mira la mia reina,
behold her between two cruel executioners,	mirala in mezzo a duo ministri crudi
her eyes fixed upon heaven.	con gli occhi fissi al cielo.
Oh, the cross hangs on her chest!	Ahi, che la croce ha sovra 'l petto affissa!
Behold how she kisses it!	Vedi or come la bacia:
Alas, who is there to comfort her	ohimé, chi la consola
in this horrible tragedy?	ne l'orribil sciagura?
Look how the wretched woman	Mira, misera, come
walks with languid steps!	move languida il passo:
Her weak, decrepit feet	ahi, ch'a pena la regge
barely sustain her, but her face	il debil piè cadente; ma la fronte
reveals no pain or fear![171]	nulla scopre di doglia o di paura.
Oh, royal heart, oh, soul	Ahi regio cor, ahi alma
adorned with noble virtue!	d'alta virtute ornata!
Alas, she looks at me!	Ohimé, ch'ella mi guarda:
What pain must seize her, the poor woman,	deh, qual dolor deve assalirla, lassa,
in seeing her dear servants abandoned,	in veder care serve abbandonate,
and herself walking towards death!	e sé sul passo de la morte, ohimé!
MACE BEARER: Move aside:	MAZZIERO: Traetevi in disparte:
leave the passage open	lascisi aperto il varco
for who comes and who follows.	a chi viene, a chi segue.

171 Again a reference to her compromised health, in context of her now entire acceptance of her fate.

CHORUS: Let me come close
and help my queen, or at least
let me touch her, let me see her, alas!
Queen, where do you go?

QUEEN: I go to life,
daughters, and before I go
I come to see you again.
I was granted this grace before dying.
I would be lucky if,
as happily as my eyes see you now,
I should also see you in a different state!
Heaven forbids me this;
but perchance it will not forbid you to see each other again
where you once saw me.
This last hope remains in my heart.
Be peaceful:
and if my pain hurts you,
sweeten your sorrow
with your freedom:
with that freedom
which you would not have had
with me.
Let this be the thanks that I owe you
for so long serving me, for braving
so many ills with me.
Your brothers and fathers
will take better care of you

than your queen
ever could.
Forgive, my daughters,
the distress, the grief
you suffered for a woman

CORO: Lascia ch'io m'avvicini
ad aiutar la mia reina, o almeno
a toccarla, a vederla, ohimiei, ohimiei!
Reina, ove ne vai?

REINA: Io me ne vo a la vita,
figlie, e anzi ch'io vada,
ritorno a rivedervi:
questa grazia m'è data in sul partire.
Fortunata, se come
vi veggon volentieri questi occhi miei,
così vi vedessi anco in altro stato!
Questo a me toglie il Cielo;
ma a voi non torrà forse il rivedervi,
ove pria me vedeste:
quest'ultima speranza al cor mi resta.
Rimanetevi in pace,
e se 'l mio mal vi duole,
raddolcite il dolore
con la libertà vostra;
con quella libertade,
che voi non eravate
per aver meco mai.
Questa fie la mercé che dar vi debbo
di tanta servitù, di tanti mali

meco passati e corsi.
I fratei vostri, i padri
avran di voi più aventurosa cura,
ch'aver non ha potuto
una vostra reina!
Perdonate, mie figlie,
i disagi sofferti,
le fatiche, gli affanni,

who can reward you for it so poorly!	per donna, che sì mal può darne il merto!
My will and hope would have been different:	Altra era la mia voglia e la speranza:
God wants it another way.	a Dio piace altrimente.
CHORUS: Oh, God, merciful God,	CORO: O Dio, pietoso Dio,
let her live	lasciala solo in vita
and double my sorrows!	e raddoppia in me i mali!
QUEEN: Turn your prayers	REINA: Volgete pure i preghi
to asking for my peace,	a chiedermi la pace,
of which I had so little on earth	sì poco avuta in terra
and have not at all deserved	e nulla meritata
where I hope to have it: in heaven.	dov'io la spero, in Cielo.
And among your prayers, let it be your care	E fra i preghi anco vostra cura sia
(this is the extreme favour	(questa è la grazia estrema
that I ask of you, dear friends and daughters)	ch'io vi dimando, amiche e figlie care)
that these bones, which you once loved,	che quest'ossa, da voi amate un tempo
and still, I believe, love,	e amate, credo, ancora,
receive a proper burial	abbian con opra pia la sepoltura
from your pious hands; this will be dear to me	da le man vostre; a me fie l'opra cara
even when I am dead bones.	anco ne l'ossa estinte.
Take them with you,	Traetele con voi,
wherever the goodly care of our Lord and God	là dove vi trarrà benigna cura
may take you.	del Signor nostro e Dio.
My lady-in-waiting,	La cameriera mia,
whom I leave I know not how,	ch'io lascio non so come,
will be your guide and protection:	sia vostra guida e scorta:
honour her, I entreat you, and abide	onoratela, prego, e ubidite
by her advice. She is benign and wise,	ai suoi consigli. Ella è benigna e saggia,
and loves you like a mother.	e v'ama quasi madre:

Love her, too,
and see in her, who remains with you,
myself, once your queen,
who abandons and leaves you.
Be mindful
that I was your mistress by nature,
your mother by affection,
and your companion by fate
of misfortunes and sorrows.[172]

CHORUS: Alas, alas!
Let my tears be an answer
if words fail.
Alas, alas, alas!

EARL OF CUMBERLAND: You've said enough: now go,
why delay further?

QUEEN: Friend, I go:
but who will help my limbs
proceed with my infirm step? I can no more.[173]

BUTLER: Oh, queen, oh, mistress!

QUEEN: Still you suffer after such long pain?
What happens, my faithful one? What do you feel?
Give me your arm, and let this be
the last act

amatela anco voi
e rimirate in lei che con voi resta,
me, già vostra reina,
che v'abbandono e lascio.
Ricordevoli siate
ch'io fui vostra padrona per natura,
ma per affetto madre
e per sorte compagna
di sventure e d'affanni.

CORO: Ahimiei, ahimiei!
Per me risponda il pianto,
se non può la parola.
Ohimé, ohimé, ohimé!

C. di COMBERLANDA: Assai s'è detto; vanne!
Che più qui si ritarda?

REINA: Amico, io vado;
ma chi le membra aita,
sì che il piè infermo vada? I' più non posso.

MAGGIORDUOMO: Ahi, reina, ahi padrona!

REINA: Dopo sì lungo strazio ancor ti duoli?
Che hai, fedel? Che senti?
Porgimi 'l braccio, e sia
questa l'opera estrema

172 Her customary ternary self-portrayal (mistress, mother, companion) is proposed again, here, in entirely positive terms, since it refers solely to her damsels and their female bond.

173 The sciatica, for which she requests the Butler's assistance. See Sartorio Loschi's *Letter* (Appendix).

of your dear, beloved but ill-rewarded service.	de la tua servitù cara e amata, ma mal guiderdonata.
EARL OF PEMBROKE: Give her your arm, help your weak mistress.	C. di PEMBROCIA: Porgile il braccio, aiuta la debil tua padrona.
BUTLER: Oh, the cruel duty of an unfortunate servant, unfortunate and faithful. I bring you, my queen, I bring you to death.	MAGGIORDUOMO: Ahi, ufficio crudele di sventurato servo, sventurato e fedele! Io, dunque, ti conduco, o mia reina, ti conduco a la morte!
QUEEN: Come, my dear, come with me. Nothing you can do is more welcome than what you are doing now. You always walked with me throughout my life, whether good or bad; now walk with me also towards death, and as you walk move your tongue with me and pray for my virtue and endurance in such a horrible passing.[174]	REINA: Vieni, caro, vien meco. Nulla più potrai far, che caro sia, se non questo ch'or fai. Sempre m'accompagnasti nel corso de la vita o buona o ria; accompagnami or anco nel passo de la morte, e movi con il piè la lingua meco, e pregami virtute e sofferenza, in così orribil varco.
BUTLER: Oh, my chest clenches and I can do nothing but suffer. Tears and wailing are, alas, my prayers!	MAGGIORDUOMO: Ahi, che 'l petto si serra, ned altro posso, ohimé, se non dolermi! Lagrime e pianto, ohimé, sono, ahi, sono miei prieghi!

174 This is the Queen's last direct appearance in the play. Going forward, her words will be reported by the Butler.

CHORUS: She goes, sisters,
and with her go these eyes and this heart,
which follows her with the eyes.
Still I see her, still:
still I see her head,
still I see her veil.[175]
Oh, she is hidden from me!
Oh, my sun has vanished!

LADY: Where, where goes my queen?
Where goes her soul?
Where is she taken by greedy, impious hands?[176]
I go behind her, I follow her,
I go to die with her.
Alas, my weak and infirm feet,
how slowly you lead me!
Alas, my powerful sorrow,
how fast you push me!

CHORUS: Oh, mother, oh, dear mother,
your acts are faithful, but superfluous:
only pain is left for us
of what we once had.

LADY-IN-WAITING: Death is left for us,
which should have come before;
but it will not be too late
if we die with her.

CHORUS: Let us die: but who will kill us,

CORO: Ella sen va, sorelle,
e seco van questi occhi e questo core,
che con gli occhi la segue.
Ancor la veggio, ancora;
ancor la testa miro,
ancor ne veggio il velo...
Ahi, ch'ella mi s'è ascosa,
ahi, ahi, sparito è 'l sole!

CAMERIERA: Dove, dove sen va la mia reina?
Dove l'anima mia?
Dove la trae mano rapace ed empia?
Dietro le vo, la seguo,
e vo seco a morire.
Ahi, piè debile e infermo,
come lenta mi scorgi!
Ahi, mio forte dolore,
come ratta mi spingi!

CORO: O madre, o cara madre,
fedel è l'opra, ma soverchia certo:
di quanto avemmo un tempo
sol ci resta il dolore.

CAMERIERA: E ci resta il morire,
ch'esser prima devea;
ma non fie tardo or anco,
morremo con lei.

CORO: Moriam, ma chi ci occide,

175 The anaphora ("Still […] / still […] / still […]") indicates the Chorus' processing of the separation.

176 Another anaphora ("Where […] / where […] / where […]"), signalling the Lady-in-Waiting's distress.

if sorrow will not?	se 'l dolor non ci occide?
But hear the laments	Ma senti che risuona
that fill the air ... It's done, it's done!	l'aria di tristi lai... è fatto, è fatto!
The cruel blow was stricken,	Fatto è 'l colpo crudele,
I felt it in my soul.[177]	l'ho sentito ne l'alma.
She is no more, my queen is no more:	Non è più, non è più la mia reina,
she left me, she departed!	m'ha lasciato, è partita!
And what horrid sight	E qual orrido aspetto
of the cruel executioner	di ministro crudele
do I see in that window,	veggio a quella fenestra,
who entreats me to look?	che m'accenna ch'io miri?
EXECUTIONER: Long live Elizabeth, most noble queen,	CARNEFICE: Viva Isabella, altissima reina,
and long may she reign! May those who dare	e lungo corso regni! E caggia e pera
to act against her, her just decrees,	in questa forma, chi d'oprar presume
and her just laws, fall and die	contra lei, contra i suoi giusti decreti
in such a way![178]	e le sue giuste leggi!
CHORUS: Oh, what do my eyes see,	CORO: Ahi, che veggion questi occhi,
oh, what does the cruel man show me?	ahi, che mi mostra il crudo!
Her head, alas, her head,	La testa, ahimé, la testa,
her beloved, dear head.	la testa amata e cara!
I recognize her, alas,	Riconoscola, ahimé,
though stained with death	se ben tinta di morte
and with her face eyeless.[179]	e senza occhi la fronte.

177 Their connection is so profound that the Chorus feels that Mary has died even without witnessing her death.

178 Durante reads these lines as in direct opposition to the ones previously spoken by the Butler ("Mary of Scotland dies, and Elizabeth / of England kills her!" vv. 1682–3). See Durante, "La Maria Stuarda dellavalliana," 364.

179 The violent, gory detail of her severed head is left to speech, rather than visuals. While Aristotle did not explicitly recommend against showing violence on stage in the *Poetics*, it became a long-standing notion that such displays should be avoided, which Della Valle clearly endorses.

Oh, dark sight! I fall, I no longer can bear the pain. Oh, the Lady-in-Waiting falls down stunned. Harm upon harm is added, and pain upon pain, if my desperate heart can feel any more pain. Help her, rescue her, let us take her inside. It is best if I sit down and hold her head in my lap.[180]	Ahi, vista tenebrosa! I caggio, io più non posso sostener il dolore. Ahi, che la cameriera sen cade tramortita: danno a danno s'aggiunge e dolore a dolore; s'altro dolor sentire può 'l disperato core. Aiutala, soccorri, o portiamla là entro. È meglio ch'io m'assida e 'l capo prenda in grembo.
BUTLER: I live, alas, I live!	MAGGIORDUOMO: Io vivo, lasso, io vivo;
My life lives, and yet it saw the death of my queen![181] Cruel me, cruel heavens. Cruel me, if pity could not, in such a painful moment, break, tear my heart; cruel heavens, which kept me alive so long to witness such great pain.	vive la vita mia, e vedut'ha la morte de la reina mia! Crudel io, crudo il Cielo! Crudel io, se pietà non ha potuto in così acerbo caso spezzar, romper il core; crudo il Ciel, che tant'anni m'ha serbato a sì grave dolore!
CHORUS: Alas, alas, alas!	CORO: Ohimiei, ohimiei, ohimiei!
Wretched me, if you see these eyes and this face: you will have proof that we feel well the pain you feel.	Meschina me! Se miri questi occhi e questa fronte, testimonio vedrai che ben sentiamo il dolor che tu senti.
BUTLER: But you feel less,	MAGGIORDUOMO: Ma tanto meno senti,

180 This image echoes the composed naturalism of Michelangelo's *Pietà*, the marble sculpture of the Virgin Mary holding the dead body of Christ on her lap.

181 The eyewitness arrives to give a detailed report of the events.

if you saw less.	quanto hai veduto meno.
The evil unseen	Ahi, che non visto male
is only half evil![182]	è sol metà di male!
CHORUS: I feel as much pain as any heart can;	CORO: Dolor sent'io, quanto sentir può un core;
but if you think that it can grow	ma se stimi che cresca
by seeing evil, paint with words	veduto mal, dipingimi parlando
the horrible event for me.	l'orribile accidente.
Words are images of things,	Son le parole imagin de le cose,
and through the images perhaps	e ne l'imagin forse
I shall feel what you truly felt.[183]	sentirò quel che tu nel ver sentisti.
LADY-IN-WAITING: Oh, wretched me!	CAMERIERA: Ohimé, misera e trista!
I see you again, oh heaven,	I' ti riveggio, o cielo,
I see you again, enemy	ti riveggio nemico
to my desires.	d'ogni mia voglia.
CHORUS: Mother!	CORO: Madre!
Come back to your senses, mother:	Torna, madre, in te stessa;
take heart, take courage!	prendi cor, prendi spirto.
LADY-IN-WAITING: Both were taken from me	CAMERIERA: E l'uno e l'altro
by her death.	m'ha tolto l'altrui morte.
Let me die!	Deh, lasciami morire!
Who are you helping?	A chi porgi tu aita?
Someone who is nothing anymore?	A chi non è più nulla?
CHORUS: Rather, you are our guide,	CORO: Anzi, sei nostra guida,

182 This commonplace assumption could also be regarded as a metatheatrical consideration: is Mary's martyrdom rendered less impactful by its being told, rather than shown? The Chorus seems to at least partially object, by reclaiming the power of words.

183 Art is the representation of truth, and words are its instruments, in this circumstance: by the same token, both the Chorus and the audience are about to feel the same pain endured by the Butler.

you are our mother and mistress,
and our queen.[184]

BUTLER: Lift, oh ancient woman,
your weak limbs;
rise and hear.

LADY-IN-WAITING: What can you tell me,
if not that I have reason, alas,
that I have reason to die?

BUTLER: I bring you other things
from she who used to be your mistress in life:
now, in dying, she prayed.

LADY-IN-WAITING: Dear praying woman,
where are you, where did you go?
But what, alas, what do you pray?
That I follow you, that I
come after your beloved steps?
I will, my queen,
I will, dear soul.

BUTLER: Resting on my arm,
as you saw her leaving here,
with her left hand, or rather
with her whole body, which could hardly
stand by itself, she climbed a long staircase. And in climbing,

sei nostra madre e donna,
e sei nostra reina.

MAGGIORDUOMO: Solleva, o donna antica,
le membra abbandonate!
Sollevati e ascolta.

CAMERIERA: Deh, che mi puoi tu dire,
se non ch'ho ragion, lassa,
ho ragion di morire?

MAGGIORDUOMO: Altre cose t'apporto
da chi solea già commandarti viva:
or morendo ha pregato.

CAMERIERA: Ahi, cara pregatrice,
dove sei, dove andasti?
Ma che, lassa, che preghi?
Ch'io ti segua, ch'io venga
per le tue orme amate?
Verrò, verrò, reina,
verrò, anima cara!

MAGGIORDUOMO: Appoggiata al mio braccio,
come partir di qui vista l'avete,
con la sinistra mano, anzi con tutte
le membra, che da sé si reggean male,
salito ha lunga scala. E in salendo,

184 The Chorus seems eager to bestow upon the Lady-in-Waiting all of the roles that the Queen's death has left vacant.

with a low voice, but high affection	con bassa voce, ma con alto affetto
in her sighs,	espresso nei sospiri,
she prayed and beseeched the Father and the Son,	pregava e invocava il Padre e 'l Figlio,
reminding them of the infinite piety,	lor rimembrando la pietà infinita,
the eternal goodness, the blood and harsh death,	la bontà eterna, il sangue e l'aspra morte
and the merits of the Mother,	e i merti de la Madre,
who was ever Virgin.[185] Then, she reached	che fu Vergine Sempre. Indi salita
the cruel room and saw	a la sala crudel, veduto ha incontro
the horrible device. It rose high	orribile apparecchio: alto s'ergeva
I know not how much, enclosed	per non so quanti gradi, intorno cinto
and wrapped in dark, black drapes,	e coperto di panni oscuri e neri,
a catafalque, and amid two big torches	un catafalco, e 'n mezzo a duo gran faci
hung a large, shiny blade from a thin rope,	pendea da sottil corda, infra due legni
between two blocks of wood. She paused	ampio ferro lucente. Èssi fermata
a while to look at it; then she turned	alquanto a rimirar; indi, rivolta
to me, who had no spirit or blood	a me, che non avea spirto né sangue
and who trembling held her: "Here is," she said,	e la reggea tremante: — Eccoti — ha detto —
"the royal pomp and seat of the queen	la real pompa e 'l seggio di reina
of two great kingdoms at once.[186] Such is the will,	di duo gran regni a un tempo. Così piace,
my friend, of He who created me, and let it be so.	amico, a Chi creommi, e così sia.
Let me go and sit there. You, grow strong	Andiamcene a sedervi. Tu rinforza

185 Mary turns her dying thoughts to the Virgin Mary, the mother of Christ.

186 She echoes her very first speech, where she had introduced herself as once a queen with two sceptres and two crowns.

in your pain with my will: help my soul
with your prayers, and with your arms the weight
of these tired, weak limbs."

In saying this, she walked, and having reached
the foot of the cruel tribunal, and I being unable
to further support her: "Stop here," she said,
"but even if you leave me,
may it please you to behold
the few steps that remain
for your queen.
Brother, I leave you here;
and leaving you weighs not on me
for myself, who am about to leave my life:
it weighs on me for you and many others,
whom I wished to thank not with the pain and suffering
that I see approaching. Those daughters
and my Lady-in-Waiting are dear to my heart.
Bring them my last goodbye
in my name;
tell them that I go to die
longing to see them,
longing to hold them;
and may my Lady-in-Waiting,
for how much she loved me, and how dearly
she held her queen,
she held her Mary,[187]
never abandon

nel tuo dolor con la mia voglia, e l'alma
coi preghi aita e con le braccia il peso
di queste membra languide e cadenti. —
Così dicendo, andava, e giunta al piede
del crudo tribunal, non potend'io
più sostenerla: — Qui ti ferma, — ha detto —
— s'anco tu m'abbandoni,
se ti spiace seguire
i pochi passi ancora
d'una reina tua.
Fratello, io qui ti lascio;
né mi pesa lasciarti
per me, che vo a lasciar ora la vita:
per te mi pesa e per molti altri, a cui
bramava altra mercé che doglie e danni,
ch'io veggio apparecchiarsi. Quelle figlie,
la cameriera mia, mi stanno al core.
Tu gli estremi saluti
porta loro in mio nome;
di' lor ch'io vo a morire,
bramosa di vederle,
bramosa d'abbracciarle;
e a la cameriera
che per quanto m'amò, per quanto cara
ebbe la sua reina,
ebbe la sua Maria,
giamai non abbandoni

187 A very touching moment, in which she highlights the coexistence of her two natures.

the daughters I abandoned,
who least deserved
to be abandoned.
May she be their counsel,
their comfort and sustenance,
if they are still kept prisoner;
and may she be their guide, if
they leave:
of this I beg her with the last of
my strength.
Remember me
in your prayers."
In saying this, she anxiously
took this letter from her bosom:
"This,"
she said, "you will give, if you
ever get there,
to my son, my blood, greatly
loved
and little enjoyed.[188] Later
you will be able to read it; let my
Lady-in-Waiting
read it with you, and let my
damsels
see it, too. May they be
satisfied with me, with what I
was able to do for them."

LADY-IN-WAITING: We see her,
we see her!
We hear the thoughts after death
of she who so sweetly would talk
to us in life.
Oh, dear letter; oh, dear
shapes by a dear hand,
how I recognize you, how I see
you,

le figlie abbandonate
da me, cui più toccava
il non abbandonarle.
Ella sia lor consiglio,
lor conforto e sostegno,
se restan prigioniere;
e sia lor guida, andando:
di ciò la prego con gli spirti
estremi.
Ricordevoli siate
di me nei vostri prieghi. —
Ciò dicendo, affannata
di sen s'è tratta questa lettra. —
Questa —
ha detto — darai tu, se mai là
giungi,
al mio figlio, al mio sangue,
molto amato
e ben poco goduto. Ad altro
tempo
la potrai legger poi; leggala
teco
la cameriera e sia veduta
ancora
da le mie damigelle. Restin esse
sodisfatte di me, con l'opra ch'io
potuto ho far per loro. —

CAMERIERA: Veggiamla, ahimé,
veggiamla!
Sentiamo ragionar dopo la morte
chi così dolce ci parlava in vita.
Ahi, cara carta! Ahi, care
forme di cara mano,
come vi conosch'io, come vi
veggio,

188 In actuality, by this time Mary was definitely bitter towards her son, whom she felt had not fought enough for her liberation. See Guy, *My Heart*, 500.

tearful and longing to see
the hand that depicted you!
You read, as I cannot
for my sight is too weak.

BUTLER: I can't see well either,
my eyes are swollen with tears
for such terrible memory.
Yet I will read as best as I can:
"Your mother dies, my son,
and in dying she writes you:
take these letters instead of my words,
and let this paper be my hand,
which I would gladly give you in dying.
You know how I die, and who kills me.
From me, know this:
that I die happy, for I see

this is the will
of He who gave me life.
I am only sorry
to not see you, and to leave you
too young and in a treacherous kingdom.
But strengthen your soul, and remember
the blood from whence you came.
Prayers and humility before God
will be the counsel and power

for your remaining strength.
Forgive those who offend me: do this
for my womb, for the breast

that I first offered you;
I do not ask for vengeance,

lacrimosa e bramosa di vedere
la man che vi dipinse!
Leggi tu, ch'io non posso,
sì debil è la vista.

MAGGIORDUOMO: Ned a me resta lume,
tanto s'empion di lagrime questi occhi,
con la memoria amara.
Ma pur leggerò il meglio:
— Tua madre more, o figlio,
e morendo ti scrive:
sian queste note invece di parole
e vaglia questa carta per la mano
che ti darei sì volentier morendo.
Com'io mora il saprai, e chi m'occida;
da me sol sappi questo,
ch'io moro consolata, poiché veggio
esser questa la voglia
di Chi mi diè la vita.
Restami sì la doglia
di non poter vederti e di lasciarti
giovane troppo d'anni e 'n regno infido;
ma tu rinforza l'alma e ti rimembri
il sangue onde nascesti.
I preghi e l'umiltade inanzi a Dio
ti varran per consiglio e saran forza
a le tue forze inferme.
Perdona a chi m'offende: ciò ti chieggio
per le viscere mie, per quella mamma,
che ti porsi primiera;
vendetta io non la chiamo,

nor does the blood that I now spread
on the ground: I'm innocent
but too sinful before heaven.

Should it ever come to you, please welcome
my little family,[189] which with me endured
so long misery and many sorrows,
and let your house be their house, and remember
that my faithful servants deserve mercy
and rest from anguish. For a long time
they lived starved of goods and food:
may your hand now see to both,
and generously. My daughters,
for such are those who are with me,
noble damsels, I entrust to you
as my flesh and blood.
See
to their virginity, their titles, their merits,
their nobility. Let them take husbands
among the first men of your king-dom; and take care
of them as sisters, as if they came out
of me, who am your mother."

CHORUS: Oh, sweet care

né la chiede quel sangue ch'ora spargo
innocente a la terra,
ma peccatrice troppo inanzi al Cielo.

La famigliuola mia, che meco dura
in sì lunghe miserie e 'n tanti affanni,
s'a te mai torna, tu l'accogli e sia
loro albergo il tuo albergo, e ti sovenga
che fida servitù chiama mercede
e 'l travaglio riposo. Lungamente
visser di ben digiuni, anzi di cibo:
la tua mano or adempia e l'uno e l'altro,
e adempia realmente. Le mie figlie,
ché tali son queste che restan meco
nobili damigelle, a te commetto,
come mie carni e sangue. Tu provvedi
a la verginitade, ai gradi, ai merti,
a la nobiltà loro: abbian mariti
i primi del tuo regno; e prendi cura
di lor, qual di sorelle e come uscite
da me, che son tua madre. —

CORO: Ahi, dolce cura

189 The *vezzeggiativo* "famigliuola" highlights the deep connection between the Queen and her servants.

from the sweetest, most beloved queen,
how you sharpen my anguish
by showing me the dear, maternal affection
of a lost mistress!

BUTLER: "My lady-in-waiting, who is only left
with a shadow of life,
I also entrust to you, my son, and leave you
in my stead. Honour her,
and let her have that power over your heart
that I had, by praying and begging; this will be enough
to show you what I wish; make it known
with your actions that you understand
more than I say. I would write more,
if I could,
so as to reason longer with you,
my dearest image;
but He who calls me to life
takes away my pen.
I will stop writing and go to die:
you, live and reign, my son,
live and reign happily and pray for me.
This heart embraces you
with what little strength it has left.
And this hand blesses you, and asks
that you not leave unburied
or buried in a foreign land,

di reina dolcissima e amata,
come inacerbi in me, lassa, l'affanno,
con mostrarmi materno e caro affetto
di padrona perduta!

MAGGIORDUOMO: — La cameriera mia, cui sol rimane
imagine di vita,
ti raccomando, o figlio, anzi ti lascio
invece di me stessa. Tu l'onora,
e possa nel tuo cuor quel ch'io potrei,
pregando e supplicando; questo basti,
per mostrar quel ch'io bramo: tu dichiara
con gli effetti ch'intendi
più assai di quel ch'io dico. Scriverei
vie più, se più potessi,
per ragionar più lungamente teco,
o mia sembianza cara;
ma mi toglie la penna
chi mi chiama la vita.
Di scriver lascio e me ne vo a morire;
tu vivi e regna, o figlio,
vivi e regna felice, e per me prega.
T'abbraccia questo core
con questo poco spirto che gli resta;
e questa man ti benedice e chiede
che non lasci insepolte,
o sepolte non lasci in terra altrui,

these bones of which you are a part: let your mother	quest'ossa onde sei parte: a te ritorni
return to you deceased, if alive she cannot.	tua madre estinta, se non può vivendo.
These are my final requests, which come to you	Questo sia 'l prego estremo, il qual sen viene
with my final kiss on your dear forehead,	col bacio estremo a quella fronte cara
which I loved myself."	ov'io amava me stessa. —
LADY-IN-WAITING: Oh, letter, oh, words,	CAMERIERA: Ahi lettera, ahi parole,
oh, sorrow, oh, sorrow!	ahi dolore, ahi dolore!
I live, I still live,	Io vivo, dunque vivo,
and she who wanted so much for me,	e morì, morì, lassa,
who loved me so much	chi tanto per me volse,
died, she died, alas!	chi m'amò tanto, ahimé!
But tell me, what more did she do?	Ma dimmi: che più fece?
What more did she say, what did she speak?	Che più parlò? Che disse?
This old woman learned from her own mouth	Seppe da la tua bocca
what she did while living;	questa vecchia quant'ella fe' vivendo;
let her learn from your tongue	sappia da la tua lingua
what she did while dying.	quel ch'ella fe' morendo.
Nothing, nothing shall be concealed	Nulla, nulla si taccia
about the final movements	dei movimenti estremi
of that beloved life.	di quella vita cara.
BUTLER: I will say all I can, to appease	MAGGIORDUOMO: Dirò quanto potrò, per compiacerti
your bitter desire.	in voglia così amara.
But already sorrow prevails, in remembering;	Ma già 'l dolor mi vince rimembrando;
what will happen, in speaking?	or che sarà parlando?
I took the letter,	La lettera ho pres'io,
tearful and trembling, and she relied	lagrimoso e tremante, ed ella ha fatto

on my arm to climb
the first step of that horrible stage,[190]
where she could barely lift her foot.
Thus, she was taken by two men close to me,
and, resting on them, without speaking further,
she reached the top, with heavy and unstable steps,
but with her brows high and content. Once there,
she left the helping hangmen and turned
in a majestic and sweet fashion
her royal face towards the many people gathered
in the heinous chamber, and who filled it
with whispers – some sighing, some laughing,[191]
some speaking painful, sad words.
She turned around and stopped and lifted her right hand,
as a sign of wanting to speak. At once a horrid,
wistful silence ensued, and the chamber seemed
empty.[192] Gathering her strength from the bottom
of her bosom, with a lovely voice
she began to say what I cannot repeat,

forza sopra il mio braccio per salire
il primo grado de l'orribil scena,
dove a pena ha potuto alzar il piede.
Così l'han presa duo più a me vicini,
e appoggiata a lor, senz'altro dire,
è giunta al sommo, con piè grave e infermo,
ma con fronte alta e lieta. Ivi condotta,
lascia i ministri aiutatori e volge
in dolce e maestevole maniera
il real volto a' molti, ond'era colma
la scelerata stanza; e di bisbiglio
l'empiean, qual di sospiri e qual di riso,
qual di parole dolorose e triste.
Rivolta e ferma alquanto, alza la destra:
di voler dir accenna. Tosto sorge
silenzio orrido e mesto, e vuota sembra
la sala. Ella, traendo dal profondo
del sen gli spirti, con soave voce
incomincia quel ch'io ridir non posso,

190 The Italian "scena" is, like the English "stage," clearly metatheatrical.

191 Laughter is yet another sign of the cruelty of the heretics gathered to witness the spectacle.

192 She is a queen even in this final moment of suffering. The effect of her voice and speech is also highlighted in Sartorio Loschi's *Letter* (Appendix).

for my heart is not strong enough to move my tongue.[193]

né 'l cor basta a dar moto a questa lingua.

CHORUS: Please, speak.
My soul became like ice
for what I heard,
perhaps it will become like marble
from what you will say.

CORO: Deh, ragiona, ti prego:
fatta è l'alma di gielo
per le sentite cose;
forse diverrà marmo
per quelle che dirai.

BUTLER: I have no more life
than what is enough
for the bitter memory
of the things I saw,
of the words I heard,
which, sadly, are fixed within my soul
to stab it forever.[194]

MAGGIORDUOMO: Ahi, ch'io non ho più vita,
se non quanto mi basta
a la memoria acerba
de le vedute cose,
de l'udite parole,
che purtroppo mi stan fisse ne l'alma,
per trafiggerla ognora!

CHORUS: Speak, and pierce my heart
with the blade that wounds you.
If you die, may this fellow servant
of yours, this companion
of tears and anguish, not live either.

CORO: Parla, e passami il core
col ferro, che te fère.
Se tu muori, non viva
questa conserva tua, questa compagna
di lagrime e di danno.

BUTLER: "I believe," my dear queen said,
"I believe," she said, "that among the many
gathered here to behold my death,
there will be someone who will look with pity

MAGGIORDUOMO: — Credo, — ha detto la cara mia reina, —
— credo — ha detto — che qui fra tanti e tanti,
uniti a rimirar la morte mia,
alcun v'avrà, che con pietà risguardi

193 The effect is almost ineffable, impossible to describe. However, the Butler will overcome this limitation.

194 The soul is metaphorically given corporeal qualities.

at the cruel tragedy of my life,[195]
and at the terrible, undignified state
where I was brought; where an innocent woman
is brought, a queen
of Scotland and France, and the rightful heir
to England, where I die. To this I was taken
by another's lack of faith and by my own
great credulity; if credulous may be called
a woman who believes a woman,
whom she prays and begs,
and a queen who believes a queen,
who promises and swears,
and a niece who believes an aunt,
whom she never offended, but always
loved and honoured.[196] And truly
faith is never certain on earth,
for that bosom lacks the faith
that was so firmly promised me. Yet,
what good is it to say this? Or rather, what good
is it to feel sorry at the stage where I am,
where it is time to die? Merciful God,
pardon the offender and the offended,

la tragedia crudel de la mia vita
e lo stato terribile e indegno,
ov'io sono condotta; ov'è condotta
una donna innocente, una reina
e di Scozia e di Francia, e giusta erede
d'Inghilterra, ov'io moro. A ciò m'han tratta
la poca fede altrui e la mia molta
credulità; se credula può dirsi
donna che crede a donna,
la qual prega e scongiura;
e reina a reina,
la qual promette e giura;
e nepote, che crede ad una zia
non offesa giamai, ma sempre amata
e onorata sempre. E veramente
non ha la fé luogo sicuro in terra,
poi ch'a me manca quella fé in quel petto
ch'a me sì ferma la promise. Pure,
il ridirlo che giova? O pur, che giova
il dolersi nel punto ov'io mi trovo,
in cui convien morir? Iddio pietoso
a chi offende perdoni e a l'offesa,

195 Again, meta-theatrical lexicon. The proclamation of innocence, as Durante remarks, takes place both out of the scene (to the people gathered to see the execution) and in the scene (to the Chorus and audience). See Durante, "La Maria Stuarda dellavalliana," 356–7.

196 The usual speech returns, always articulated in three parts.

which I am. But how rightfully,	la qual son io. Ma quanto giustamente,
you judge it yourselves: hear my faults!	le colpe udite e giudicatel voi.
Your queen orders my death	Mi fa dar morte la reina vostra,
because, she says, I skilfully tried	perch'io, dice, ho tentato e arti e modi
to take her life, and because I then	di privarla di vita e perch'io poi
did all I could to get out of the place where	ho fatto ogni opra per uscir di dove
she keeps me prisoner. On this horrible,	ella chiusa mi tiene. Per quel passo
final step, where I see myself,	orribile ed estremo, ove mi veggio,
which will soon take me to hear	che fra poco ha da trarmi a udir il giusto
the rightful Judge of life and death	Giudice de la vita e de la morte
to receive either eternal glory or eternal punishment,	per aver gloria eterna o eterna pena,
I swear to you, my friends, that the first fault	vi dico, amici, che la prima colpa
is fake and false. I never devised	è finta e falsa. Io nulla mai pensai
her death nor did I ever wish for it.	de la sua morte, né giamai la volsi.
I confess to the other fault, if it is a fault	L'altra colpa confesso, s'è pur colpa
that a queen, a free lady,	ch'una reina, libera signora,
to whom God gave no other judge	a cui giudice alcun non diede Iddio,
besides Himself,[197] imprisoned	se non se stesso, fatta prigioniera
by who least should, should try to flee	da chi men deve, di fuggir procura
her miserable prison, whose harshness	miserabil prigione e dura, quanto
you cannot conceive. If this is a fault,	non potete stimar: se questa è colpa,
then I die rightfully convicted.	io moro giustamente condennata.

197 In this final speech, Mary reinforces all of the concepts that she had already proposed earlier, including her divine right.

But whether my death is fair or unfair
– but it truly is not fair – I die satisfied
and happy, for I know that the real reason
for my death is my being faithful
to my Lord. The faith that was promised
in the holy water,[198] where heavenly grace washes
away all stains, I keep pure and whole,
and recognize the highest authority of the Holy See
on earth, where the Roman pontiff
unties and ties and opens and closes heaven.
In this faith I lived, and in it I die.
This I proclaim and reaffirm, and I long
for my blood, and I am pleased it will be my testimony.[199]

Thus, I die happy. If there is among you
someone who shares the same feeling,
I beg you pray for me and in any place
and any time bear witness
that Mary Stuart[200] dies a queen,
obedient to what sacred Rome and its holy Lord

Ma giusta o ingiusta la mia morte sia,
che giusta non è inver, io sodisfatta
moro e contenta; poiché so che vera
cagion de la mia morte è l'esser io
fedele al mio Signor. La fé promessa
ne l'acque sacre, ove ogni macchia lava
Grazia celeste, pura e intiera serbo
e somma autorità confesso in terra
il Santo seggio, onde 'l roman Pastore
e scioglie e lega e apre e chiude il Cielo.
In questa fede vissi, in questa moro:
ciò protesto e confermo, e 'l sangue mio
bramo e m'è car che testimon ne sia.

Così moro ben lieta. Voi, s'alcuno
v'è pur fra voi, ch'abbia il medesmo senso,
prego preghi per me, e 'n ogni luogo
in ogni tempo testimonio renda
che Maria Stuarda muor reina
ubidiente a quel ch'impera e insegna

---

198 The holy water of her baptism.

199 The noun she uses here, "testimony" ("testimonio"), etymologically has the meaning of martyrdom, from the Greek μαρτύριον.

200 This is the first time, at the close of her life, in which she identifies herself.

command and teach.
I am ready to die."

CHORUS: May God accept your blood,
oh, martyr queen,[201]
for His glory and yours!
And since it is certain,
I should rejoice with you;
but too great, too great is the pain
of remaining here without you, my commander,
my support and comfort.

BUTLER: This soul is reinvigorated
by thinking that she now blessedly sits
among the blessed people.
As she finished speaking these words,
she turned to her punishment
and, looking at the blade,
she paused a little, and looked horrified;
and in the midst of her horror, she turned her eyes
to heaven, so fixed they were that it seemed like
she would have wanted to fix herself into heaven.
A loud sigh marked the end of this brief rapture.
And she moved like a man[202]
who has just awoken,
and, clenching her cross

Roma sacrata e il Signor suo santo.
Ed eccomi a morire. —

CORO: Accetti Dio 'l tuo sangue,
o martire reina,
a sua gloria e a tua!
La qual poich'è sicura,
teco allegrarmi, teco, ahimé, devrei;
ma troppo, troppo è 'l danno
di restar io qui senza te, mia duce,
mio sostegno e conforto!

MAGGIORDUOMO: Prende vigor quest'alma
in pensar ch'ella siede ora beata
fra le genti beate.
Giunta al fine di queste sue parole,
s'è rivolta al supplicio,
e rimirando il ferro,
fermata alquanto, è parsa inorridirsi;
e fra l'orror gli occhi ha rivolti al cielo,
sì fissi che parea che 'n ciel volesse
figger anco se stessa. Alto sospiro
è stato il fin del breve rapimento,
e s'è mossa qual uom che 'l sonno lassi,
e serratasi al petto

---

201 The theme of martyrdom is, as we have seen, entirely explicit here.
202 The gender dynamics of this simile are probably not casual: after the initial horror in dealing with the sight of the blade, her ensuing courage is similar to that of a man.

to her bosom, which she always kept
in her right hand, with her left hand
she began to loosen her dress from around
her neck and, once she did, she folded it back.
But since she could not do it easily
by herself, the cruel executioner
stuck out his hand to help her, and she said:
"Friend, this is not for you.
A less filthy hand should do it."[203]

CHORUS: Oh, royal blood,
how you keep your noble, highest spirit
even upon dying!

BUTLER: Aside on the horrid stage[204]
was a woman,
the wife, I believe, of one of the guards;
she turned to her, and with a benign attitude
and the trace of a smile on her lips,
"Sister," she said, "please take on the
trouble of helping me die; I beg you, fold
my dress and the veil that wraps my throat,

la croce, che pur sempre ha ritenuto
ne la man destra, con la manca mano
ha cominciato a sciôrsi intorno al collo
la vesta, e sciolta a ripiegarla indietro.
Né potendolo far agevolmente
da se medesma, il manigoldo fiero
stesa ha la man, per aiutarla; ed ella:
— Amico, ha detto, questo a te non tocca.
Mano men lorda il faccia. —

CORO: O regio sangue,
come ritieni in sul morir gli spirti
nobili, eccelsi!

MAGGIORDUOMO: Era sul fero palco,
in disparte, una donna,
moglie, cred'io, d'alcun dei guardiani;
a lei s'è volta, e con benigno modo,
e con la bocca tinta anco di riso:
— Sorella — ha detto — prendi tu la noia
d'aiutarmi a morir; ripiega, prego,
la vesta e 'l velo che la gola cinge,

203 Her rejection of the Executioner's touch is an important element in Sartorio Loschi's *Letter* (Appendix).

204 Metatheatrical lexicon, once again.

and let the blade have it bare."	e dàlla nuda al ferro.
The tearful	— Lagrimosa
woman moved, and stripped the beautiful neck	s'è la femina mossa e riverente
bare, with reverence.	ha nudato il bel collo...
LADY-IN-WAITING: Oh, neck, oh, throat,	CAMERIERA: Ahi collo, ahi gola,
how many times did these hands of mine adorn you	quante volte t'ornâr queste mie mani
with the whitest pearls, and how many times did I see	di bianchissime perle, e quante vidi
their whiteness being surpassed by your whiteness!	il lor candor vinto dal tuo candore!
Now a sharp blade has cut you, and dark blood	Or t'ha tronco aspro ferro e tetro sangue
is your horrid necklace.	t'è orrido monile!
BUTLER: Then, with only two steps she reached	MAGGIORDUOMO: Indi con sol duo passi s'è accostata
the terrible scythe, which generated horror	a la terribil falce, che 'n mirarla
in just seeing it, so wide and sharp it was,	spirava orror, sì ampia e sì radente,
and kneeled down. The pious woman	e ginocchion s'è posta. La pietosa
took a thin, white cloth out of her	donna, traendo da la vesta un panno
dress, folded it lengthwise	bianco, sottil, l'ha ripiegato in giro,
and, crying and trembling, tied it	e tremante e piangente sopra gli occhi
over her eyes. And while she tied the knot,	gliel'ha annodato. E mentre il nodo stringe,
my queen said: "Thanks be to God	la mia reina dice: — Grazie a Dio,
that I found someone to help me	ch'io trovo in Inghilterra chi m'aiti
and take pity on me in England. But you, sister,	e chi m'abbia pietà! Ma tu, sorella,
if such thanks, or at least a sign of a grateful	se t'è cara mercede o segno almeno
soul in an unhappy woman pleases you,	d'animo grato in infelice donna,

embrace me, I beg you. Here, I embrace you,
as a sign that your actions are dear to me;[205]
and let me die." Thus, she softly put her hands around
her neck and kissed her.

Then, she lifted her face to heaven,
paused a little and then, humbly
embracing the cross,
she stretched her neck

below the horrid scythe.[206]

CHORUS: Oh, my heart abandons me
in just imagining it!

BUTLER: In seeing her so,

the cruel executioner promptly cut off
the rope whence the mortal blade hung,[207]
which, in falling, plunged

in her white flesh, in that beautiful neck.
Thus, with her body laying down on one side
and her head on another, she remained

abbracciami, ti prego: ecco t'abbraccio
per segno che m'è cara l'opra tua;
e lasciami morir. Così le ha cinto
il collo caramente e l'ha baciata.
Quinci, alzata la fronte inverso il cielo,
s'è ferma alquanto, e umilmente poscia
abbracciata la croce, il collo ha steso
sotto l'orrida falce.

CORO: Ahi, che si parte

il cor imaginando!

MAGGIORDUOMO: Il fier ministro,
in rimirarla tale, ha tronco tosto

la corda onde pendeva il mortal ferro,
il qual precipitando s'è sommerso
ne le candide carni, in quel bel collo.
Così, stese le membra da una parte
e da l'altra la testa, ella è rimasa

205 Even in this last exchange, a female bond emerges and takes precedence: after the Lady-in-Waiting and Chorus, it is the guard's unknown wife whom Mary elects as her final companion and aide.

206 These *endecasillabi*, in the Italian original, mark the solemnity of the moment, which has reached its apex (see Gerato, "Un'anima traviata," 10–11).

207 In reality, Mary was beheaded with an axe. The instrument depicted here is similar to an ancestor of the guillotine, the Italian "mannaia," which had a half-moon-shaped blade sustained by a rope.

a trembling corpse, whence blood rushed out
in great gushes; and we saw
her sweet mouth
open and close as she drew
her final breaths, graciously
even among the fits of her horrendous death.[208]

LADY-IN-WAITING: Oh, heavens! Alas, what more pain do you keep in store.
for me, if this does not kill me?

CHORUS: You died, alas, you died,
oh, beautiful woman,
oh, sweetest and dearest one,
oh, queen, oh, mistress!
What shall we do? Where shall we go? What will it be
of this bitter life that we are left?

Let us weep, sisters,
for weeping is most fair
for those who take so many misfortunes
upon their weak shoulders.
I weep for her death,
I weep for my life,
I weep for the harsh ruin[209]
of my beloved land.
But, alas, what do I see? Here comes the banner[210]

cadavero tremante, onde si sgorga
per grosse canne il sangue; e s'è veduta
la dolcissima bocca,
con trar gli spirti estremi,
riaprirsi e serrarsi, graziosa
anco nei moti de la morte orrenda.

CAMERIERA: Ahi cielo! A qual dolor, lassa, mi serbi,
se questo non m'occide?

CORO: Moristi, ahimé, moristi,
o bellissima donna,
o dolcissima e cara,
o reina, o padrona!
Noi che farem? Dove n'andrem? Che fie
di questa amara vita che ci avanza?

Piangiam, sorelle, ohimé,
ché giustissimo è 'l pianto
di chi tante sventure insieme accoglie
sovra debili spalle.
Piango la morte altrui,
piango la vita mia,
piango l'aspra ruina
de la mia patria amata!
Ma, ahi, che veggio? Ohimiei, ecco l'insegna

208 The description is so vividly gory that the Butler, at the end, has to add that despite it all she was still as graceful as before.

209 The anaphora ("I weep […] / I weep […] / I weep […]") is used to highlight the Chrous' pain.

210 The lifeless body of the Queen.

of our misfortune,
of our ruin!
Behold over there the long, dark board
carried by four men,
covered in dark drapes: alas, this is
the beloved body
of my queen!
Pain is added to pain,
and evil replaces evil;
but I welcome this evil, if it increases the evil I feel
until the very end.
Let these eyes see the blood,
if my soul already felt the wound.
And let eyes and soul both
suffer this extreme pain.

MESSENGER: Here comes back to you, ladies, whatever can
come back to you of your mistress:[211]
we bring her back to where she left
never again to come back.
Give her your tears,
and prepare the bloodless body
for its burial.

CHORUS: The task is painful and bitter,
but due and welcome:
lay down here
that blessed charge. Where do you go?
Where to, executioner?
Stop; do not prolong the awful sight

de la nostra sventura,
de la nostra ruina!
Mira là, da quattr'uomini portata
lunga tavola oscura,
coperta a panni oscuri. Ohimè, che questo,
è questo 'l corpo amato
de la reina mia!
Dolor giunge a dolore
e mal sottentra a male;
ma caro è 'l mal, s'accresce il mal ch'io sento,
sino a l'ultimo male.
Veggian questi occhi il sangue,
se l'alma ha già sentito la ferita,
e gli occhi e l'alma insieme
abbian le doglie estreme.

MESSO: Qui torna a voi, o donne, quel che puote
a voi tornar de la padrona vostra:
colà la ritorniam, onde partissi
per non tornar più mai.
Voi le lagrime vostre
le date, e componete il corpo esangue,
perch'abbia sepoltura.

CORO: È l'ufficio aspro, amaro,
ma pur devuto e caro:
deponi qui, deponi
quell'onorato incarco. Dove vai?
Dove passi, ministro?
Ferma; non ci allungar la fiera vista

211 Her mortal body, abandoned by her immortal soul.

of someone else's cruelty
and of our sorrow!

LADY-IN-WAITING: No more,
no more let such blessed charge
be the burden of such
undeserving,
cruel shoulders.
Stop, leave us here what our
heaven
leaves us of all that is ours.

MESSENGER: Executioners, lay
down the cold body,
and leave its care
to those who must care for it.

LADY-IN-WAITING: The care of
these dear limbs
is mine:
I took care of them and adorned
them in life;
now I will cry for them and preserve them in death.

CHORUS: Lift the dark
drapes,
and let these sad, tearful
eyes see
a much darker sight.
Alas, alas, alas!

LADY-IN-WAITING: Is this how
I see you, how you come
back to me, my queen?
Cursed be the hand that gives
you back to me
in such miserable state!
Cruel is whoever took you from
me;
cruel are you, my life, for leaving
me!

de l'altrui crudeltade
e del nostro dolore!

CAMERIERA: Non più, non più
sia peso
di spalle così indegne e sì
crudeli
così onorato incarco;
ferma, lascia qui a noi quel che ci
lascia
d'ogni ben nostro il Cielo!

MESSO: Deponete, ministri, il
freddo corpo,
e lasciaten la cura
a chi ha d'averne cura.

CAMERIERA: A me la cura
tocca
di queste membra care:
io vive le trattai, vive le ornai;
or piangerolle, or serberolle
morte!

CORO: Tolgasi il panno oscuro,
e sorga agli occhi lagrimosi e
tristi
vista molto più oscura,
ohimiei, ohimiei, ohimiei!

CAMERIERA: Così dunque ti
veggio e così torni
a me, o mia reina?
Maledetta la man, che mi ti
rende
in sì misera forma!
Crudel chi mi ti tolse,
crudel tu, vita mia, che mi
lasciasti,

Cruel is me,[212] for not following
your steps, my mistress,
your end, my lady!
I remain here! I,
old, slow, infirm,
vile, wrinkled, and already unwelcome to my age,
I remain here as a burden to the earth;
and you, wise and beautiful,
beloved and dear,
you left, alas, you left us:
oh, France's past glory,
oh, Scotland's hope![213]

crudel io, che non seguo
il tuo passo, padrona,
il tuo fine, mia donna!
Io, dunque, resto! Io, dunque,
vecchia, languida, inferma,
putida, vizza e già noiosa agli anni,
resto inutile peso de la terra;
e tu saggia, tu bella,
tu sospirata e cara
partisti, ohimé, partisti,
o già gloria di Francia,
o speranza di Scozia!

CHORUS: Oh, my sustenance, oh, life
for thousands and thousands of people, alas!

CORO: O mio sostegno, o vita
di mille genti e mille, ohimiei, ohimiei!

LADY-IN-WAITING: You will get a burial
from these hands, which should have been buried
and should have become dust
long before you.
Cruel is whoever calls me
to such pitiful task:
both pitiful and odious!
I talk to you, I embrace you,
my dear queen,
and yet you don't reply,
you say nothing, alas!
Where, where is the voice
which used to comfort me?
Where are the eyes, where is the gaze
that I used to relish?

CAMERIERA: Avrai tu sepoltura
da questa man, ch'esser devea sepolta,
esser polve devea
inanzi te molt'anni:
crudel, chi mi riserba
a ufficio sì pietoso,
pietoso quanto odioso!
Ti parlo, ohimé, t'abbraccio,
o mia reina cara,
e tu nulla rispondi,
tu nulla dici, ohimé!
Dove, dov'è la voce
che solea consolarmi?
Ov'è l'occhio, ov'è il guardo
ov'io solea allegrarmi?

---

212 Yet another anaphora.

213 Scotland's – now lost – hope of religious and political restoration. On the function of Scotland in Catholic propaganda, see Villani, "From Mary."

I feel nothing, nothing
but anguish;
I see nothing, nothing
but your sorrowful, painful relics
which will always bring death to me.

CHORUS: Oh, wretched torso,
wretched remains
of a miserable lady,
how do I see in you
the worst of all evils!
Let us take, oh unhappy us, let us take
over our shoulders oppressed
by such terrible ruin
the beloved burden of a great queen.
Let us carry the dead limbs:
we who are still alive,
ministers of death,
doomed only to deal with horrors,
only to carry sorrows,
unhappy signs of an unhappy fate!

Nulla, nulla più sento,
se non, lassa, il tormento;
nulla, nulla più miro,
se non reliquia lagrimosa, amara,
da farmi morir sempre!

CORO: Ahi, miserabil tronco,
miserabil avanzo
di misera padrona,
come, come in te veggio
d'ogni gran male il peggio!
Prendiam, triste, prendiamo
sovra le spalle oppresse
da terribil ruina
il peso amato d'una gran reina;
portiamo membra morte,
noi che vive restiamo
proprie ministre a morte,
solo a trattar orrori,
solo a portar dolori,
mostri infelici d'infelice sorte!

Appendix

Letter
by Sartorio Loschi

Concerning the death of the Queen of Scots
To the illustrious Count Marcantonio Martinengo

Bergamo,
Comino Ventura, 1587[1]

Lettera
di Sartorio Loschi

Su la morte della Reina di Scotia

All'Ill. Sig. Marc'Antonio Martinengo Conte di Villa Chiara.

In Bergamo,
Per Comino Ventura, 1587

1 There is little information about Sartorio Loschi, or Loscho. He was from Vicenza and worked, Veronica Carta writes, for the Duchy of Mirandola, which was under French protection. In this capacity, he resided in Paris, where there was considerable interest in (and horror at) the death of Mary Queen of Scots. His dedicatee, Count Marcantonio Martinengo, was a man of letters and arms, whom Loschi might have met either in northern Italy or at the French court, which he, too, visited. The letter, based not on eyewitness but on second-hand information, was printed in 1587 after circulating in manuscript form. In the same year, other, slightly abridged versions of Loschi's letter were also printed in Parma and Vicenza. An exemplar of pseudo-documentary Marian propaganda, this letter clearly delineates the balance of power and culpability at work in the execution of the Catholic queen, including an explicit condemnation of Elizabeth's cunning. The letter, particularly the first part about Mary's arrival in England, draws heavily on the immensely popular chronicle by the French ambassador to England, Guillaume de l'Aubespire, Baron of Chateauneuf, itself a second-hand narrative of the events (Carta, "Alle origini," 138). For more information about the letter, its background, as well as its editorial history, see Carta, 153–8, and Phillips, *Images of a Queen*, 153–5. On the dedicatee, Count Martinengo, see Gino Benzoni, "Martinengo, Marcantonio," in *Dizionario Biografico degli Italiani*, vol. 71 (Rome: Istituto della Enciclopedia Italiana, 2008).

To the illustrious Sig. Marcantonio Martinengo
Count of Villachiara

All'Ill. Sig. Marc'Antonio Martinengo
Conte di Villa Chiara

My most excellent Lord,

Molto Mag. Mio Sig. Osservandiss.

It has been so long since I last wrote that I believe Your Lordship will surely not recognize my handwriting. I have, despite this lateness, continued to revere and respect you as I should, thinking that it would suffice me, for lack of other opportunities, to beg my brother Scipione in every letter to send you my best. But having recalled that, upon leaving you, I had promised to send you news about the things that would happen in these lands, I felt I should inform you about the miserable, tragic end of the poor Queen of Scots, one of the most beautiful women that our age ever saw. Queen of Scots by nature, of France by marriage, and of England by true succession, if reason had had its way.

Egli è tanto tempo che io non ho scritto a V.S. che credo certo, che quasi non riconoscerà più il mio carattere, ma non per quello sono restato d'amarla et osservarla sempre come devo, parendome che mi bastasse, non havendo altra occasione, di pregar per ogni mia lettera il Signor Scipione mio fratello di farli le mie raccomandationi: ma ricordandomi haverli nel partire che feci di costà promesso di darli alle volte nova delle cose che occorrevano in questi paesi, non ho voluto restar di usarli di questo miserabil et tragico fine della povera Regina di Scotia una delle più belle donne ch'habbia havuto l'età nostra. Regina di Scotia per natura, di Francia per matrimonio et d'Inghilterra per vera successione, se la ragione vi avesse avuto loco.

Your Lordship must know that while this Queen many years ago chanced to go from Scotland to France, where she was married to King Francis II, she was by evil winds carried to

V.S. deve sapere che occorrendo molti anni sono a questa Regina passar di Scotia in Francia dove era stata prima maritata al Re Francesco II fu dalla malignità de venti spinta

England's shores.[2] Although that other Queen had signed her public passport and assured her she would freely be allowed to pass through or stay, she was nonetheless imprisoned by her because of the claim that the Queen of Scots had over the Kingdom of England, where she remained for nineteen uninterrupted years. In that period, she attempted many a time to flee, and even more so, the Catholics and her followers who secretly live in that country tried to let her escape, so that the Kingdom might be given back to its true heiress and reunited with the Holy Catholic Church. This they tried with various means, mostly by plotting against the very Queen of England, as they did, among other times, four months ago; but this would take too long for me to relate.[3] They were, however, found out and seventeen of them were made to die at once. For this, the Queen of Scots was tried; but she, not knowing what to say and fearing she would hurt some of her

in porti d'Inghilterra: dove se bene con passaporto publico segnato da quella Regina era stata assicurata di poter liberamente passare et trattenersi, fu nientedimeno da lei fatta pregione: per le pretensioni et parti grande che havea detta Regina di Scotia nel regno d'Inghilterra: nella qual pregionia ha vivuto 19 anni continui. In questo tempo ella ha cercato molte volte di fuggirsene, et molto più hanno cercato li cattolici et suoi seguaci che sono segreti nel Paese di farla fuggire per rimetter quel regno nelle mani della vera successione et riunirlo alla Santa Chiesa Cattolica. Et questo l'hanno tentato con varij mezzi, et il più delle volte con il congiurar contro la Regina d'Inghilterra medesima, come fecero fra le altre quattro mesi sono, che troppo lungo faria il raccontar come: ma furono scoperti et 17 in una volta ne furon fatti morire. Per questo fu processata la Regina di Scotia, la quale non sapendo che cosa ci fusse a dire et dubitando di far preiudicio a qualcheduno

2 A simplified summary of the events of 1568, when Mary arrived in England expecting Elizabeth's protection after her forced abdication and imprisonment.

3 Loschi is referring to the Babington Plot, whose aim was to put Mary on the throne of England by assassinating Elizabeth.

servants or followers, always declined answering the judge who was interrogating her because he lacked standing, for she did not grant the Queen of England any juridical authority over another Queen such as herself. But all was for naught, and rather raised suspicion, and so they stripped her title from her and sentenced her to death. The sentence was then confirmed by England's parliament, which convened for such occasion, and nothing more was required for it to be carried out except for the Queen's signature, which she at first seemed reluctant to give, for she wanted to please the King of France, who was pressuring her not to sign. In fact, the Queen of Scots was both his sister-in-law and a good friend of the Crown. So, while his ambassador, whom the King had sent for this reason, remained in England, she refused to sign the warrant. But after he left, she signed it, and wanted to make believe that she had only done it to satisfy her people's insistence. But having given it to her secretary with the explicit indication, under penalty of death, not to publish it – for she did not in any way want the execution to be carried out – he was prompted, as it were, by the interest of the Kingdom to give it to Lord Robert, Earl of

de suoi servitori et fautori, negò sempre di voler rispondere al giudice che la interogava come incompetente, non concedendo alla Regina d'Inghilterra giuridica autorità sopra di lei similmente Regina, ma il tutto servì di nulla, anzi augumentò il suspetto, et per sentenza la desgradorno di Regina et sententiorno a morte, la qual sentenza fu poi anco da stati d'Inghilterra a questo effetto radunati confirmata, ne altro vi occorreva per esseguirla se non che fusse sottoscritta dalla regina, a che ella mostrò di rendersi nel principio molto difficile et di voler in questo gratificar il Re di Francia che gliene faceva molto instantia; si per esser la Regina di Scotia sua Cognata come anco per la buona amicitia che ha sempre avuto con quella Corona, né mai infino a tanto, che l'ambasciatore del Re mandato per questo stette in Inghilterra, la volse signare: ma doppo partito la signò et voria che si credesse che l'havesse fatto solo per sodisfare alla instanza de suoi populi, ma data però in mano al suo secretario con espressa comissione sotto pena della vita di non la publicare, non volendo in modo alcuno che si venisse all'essecutione, ma che egli mosso per quello dice del servitio del Regno senza dargliene parte l'habbia data al Milord Robert

Mestrice[4] without informing her. This man, with the help of other notables in the Kingdom, derived his authority from the above warrant and had it executed without her consent: you can believe this if you will, but the cunning of that Queen is well known. In short, on the evening of Tuesday the 17th of the past month,[5] this Lord,[6] accompanied by the man who was ordinarily in charge of surveilling the Queen of Scots,[7] went to her chamber in a castle fifty miles removed from London. They entered with the warrant in hand and, omitting the title of Queen and simply calling her Mary, told her that she already knew her sentence, and that the time had come to execute it, which would be done the following day at 11 in the morning.[8] Without showing any sign of distress, she answered that she had been waiting for this for the past three months; nevertheless, she thought it a gesture of tyranny

altrimente Conte di Mestrice il quale con l'intervento d'altri principali del Regno di propria autorità fondata sopra detta sentenza senza suo consenso l'habbino fatta eseguire: ma lo credi chi vuole che troppo chiare sono l'astuzie di quella Regina. In somma andò il Marti sera che fu alli 17 del passato il Milort in compagnia di quello che ordinariamente aveva carica di guardar la Regina di Scotia ad un suo castello lontano di Londra 50 miglia dalla camera di essa Regina, et entrati dentro con la sentenza in mano, lassando li titoli di Regina et nominandola per semplice Maria li dissero ch'ella sapeva la sentenza data contra di lei, et ch'era venuto il tempo di esseguirla, il che saria per matina seguente alle 16 hore: ella senza punto turbarsi li rispose, che erano hormai tre mesi che s'aspettava questo; se bene li pareva gran tirannia; che la Regina d'Inghilterra volesse intraprender sopra di lei,

4 Unclear who the person referred to here is. The most probable suspect would be Elizabeth's secretary of state, Robert Cecil, Earl of Shrewsbury, but for lack of certainty I will maintain the Italianate title.

5 The date according to the Julian calendar (used in England) is 7 February, but Loschi uses the Gregorian calendar (used on the Continent).

6 Loschi may be conflating different people: rather than Cecil – if that is indeed the Lord Robert mentioned previously – it was Robert Beale who visited Mary and read the warrant.

7 Possible reference to Amias Paulet.

8 Loschi speaks of "alle 16 hore," which in the Italian usage corresponded to 11 a.m. in winter months.

that the Queen of England should wish to do this to her, since she lacked the authority to do so, and had only come to seize her because of her trust. She added that she welcomed this evil as a resolution by the grace of God, which would take her out of the pain that she suffered daily and added that she would gladly welcome them back the following morning. They presented her with two bishops of their religion to assist her, but she asked whether they were Catholic and, having learned they were not, she rejected them and begged that she would be granted a Catholic priest for these last few hours in her life, and that they at least would not torment her. All of this, they say, she heard and spoke with utmost calm, peace in her soul, and serenity on her face, so much so that her ladies and servants who were present did not notice anything until, after the Lords had left, she told them herself. This caused them to weep and cry greatly, but she comforted them and exhorted them to pray to God that He might grant her strength, and spent the whole night until the break of dawn in constant prayer. And many people say that among the three servants who were with her, there was a priest whom the Pope had

che non vi haveva altra auttorità, se non quella che si prendeva per haverla nelle mani capitatavi sotto la sua fede; et che nel male riceveva per gran gratia da Iddio questa sua risolutione per uscire di tante pene in che ogni giorno viveva, et che venissero la mattina che veneriano aspettati et ben venuti. Li apresentorno doi vescovi della loro Religione per assisterla, ella li addimandò se erano Catolici, et intendendo che non, li recusò supplicandoli poi che in questo ultimo suo termine non la volevano consolar di concederli un Prete Catolico, non volessero ne anco turbarla, et tutto questo dicono fu da lei et inteso, et risposto con tanta quiete, riposo d'animo et serenità di viso, che le sue donne et servitori domestici che vi erano presenti non si accorsero di cosa alcuna, se non che doppo partiti li Milorti ella glie lo disse; onde li pianti et gridi furono grandissimi, ma ella riprendendoli li consolava et esortava a pregar Dio per lei che li desse costanza et stette tutta la notte infino appresso il giorno in continue orationi, et vi sono molti che dicono, che di tre servitori domestici che aveva seco nelle pregioni ve ne era uno prete, il quale per secreta permissione del Papa vestiva l'habito mondano, et haveva facultà in ogni luoco e

secretly allowed to wear secular clothes, and he had the ability in any place and time, as the occasion demanded, to consecrate. With this man she pretended to talk privately, and by him, it is said, she was blessed and received the eucharist through a Host that he had hidden in a handkerchief, which he had feigned giving her to dry her tears. As dawn approached, she lay in bed entirely dressed, and rested quietly for some time, and when she rose, she went back to her prayers. When the time came, she heard her chamber door open and went to meet the two Lords who had come with an Executioner dressed in velvet, with a golden chain around his neck. She told them she welcomed them, and that she had been more vigilant than them, for they had arrived one hour later than they had said the night before, and that she had two things to ask of her sister the Queen of England – using that name as a sign of friendship – but did not know whether they would be granted. One thing was that fifteen days earlier she had written a will which she wished to be sent to Scotland and executed. The other was that although those who were given such punishment were usually left alone in the end,

tempo, secondo l'occasion di poter consecrar, et che da questo mostrando di parlar seco d'altro in parte fusse confessata et comunicata, et che l'Hostia in particolar le fusse da lui presentata in un fazzoletto, mostrando di darglielo per occasione di asciugar il volto: approsimatasi l'alba si misse nel letto tutta vestita dove ripossò per un pezzo molto quietamente, et levatasi tornò all'orationi. Venuta l'hora et sentendo aprir la porta della Camera andette contro alli dui Milorti che venivano con il Carnefice vestito di velluto, con una collana d'oro al collo: li disse che fussero li ben venuti et che ella era stata piu vigilante di loro, che havevano posposto un'hora a quello dissero la sera avanti, et che aveva due cose da ricercare alla Regina d'Inghilterra sua sorella, usando questo nome d'amicitia, che non sapeva se le sariano accordate, l'una ch'ella quindeci giorni sono haveva fatto un testamento il qual deserava bene che fusse mandato in Scotia et essequito, l'altra che quelli che erano condotti a simil supplicio solevano esser abbandonati da tutti li suoi, ma che per la qualità sua ella desiderava d'esser accompagnata da le sue donne, et dalla sua poca famiglia, che l'uno e l'altro li fu promesso,

by virtue of her position she wished to be accompanied by her ladies and her few servants: both things were granted. When the Executioner approached and tried to tie her up, with royal imperiousness she ordered him not to touch her, which she repeated other times both to him and to the other ministers, and it was said that at each command they felt something which stunned them for they knew not whence it came. At last, she herself put her hand over a gentleman's shoulder, who was to support her, because the sciatica that she had gotten in prison had not been treated well and had left her with a slight limp. She exited the chamber into an antechamber and from there entered a great hall where roughly 400 people were gathered. The hall was all draped in black, and at the end there was an imposing catafalque covered in black velvet all the way down to the ground, and they say that throughout her captivity the Queen was never seen more beautiful or serene than she was during her walk towards it. Once she reached the steps of the catafalque, that gentleman wanted to leave her, but she begged him to help her, for without his help she couldn't have walked up the stairs, and told him this would be the last

et avicinandosi il Boia per legarla con un Regio Imperio li comandò che non la toccasse, il che fece anco molte altre volte et a lui et ad altri ministri, et è stato avertito che a questo Imperio sentivano dentro di se un so che, che li rendeva tutti storditi, non sapendo dove ciò procedesse. Alla fine messa ella medesima la mano sopra la spalla a Milort, che l'haveva in carica per sustegno suo essendo per una siatica venutagli in pregione et mal medicata restata un poco zoppa, uscì della camera in un anticamera, et di quella in una gran sala dove potevano esser da 400 persone, tutta tapezzata di nero, in Capo la quale era un Catafalco eminente coperto di velluto nero infino a terra, et dicono che in tutto il tempo della sua pregionia non fu mai vista la Regina ne più bella ne con più serena faccia di quello che era in questo passaggio: arrivata alla scala del Catafalco, voleva il Milort lassarla, ma ella lo pregò di agiutarla, che senza il suo agiuto non potria montare che saria per l'ultima pena che ella li fusse per dare, il che egli fece. Montata il palco si voltò alla sua adorata famiglia et driciato il ragionamento a un suo mastro di casa, come Capo li disse che li rincresceva molto di lassarli, et di non haver modo di poter riconoscer la bona et fidel servitù loro, ma

inconvenience she would do him, and he complied. Once she reached the stage, she turned to her beloved servants and, addressing one of her House masters as the head of them all, she told him she was sad to leave them, and that she had no way to compensate their good and faithful service, but that they should go and find the King, her son, instead, for he would do what she could not. And in that moment, she turned her head and lamented loudly before the people gathered, calling God as her witness, that she had never in deeds or words conspired, or consented to conspire, in any way against the Queen of England, and she prayed to God that He would forgive her if she was lying. She then turned to the House Master and asked him to send her best to her son and to beg him from her to go back to the Holy Roman Catholic Church, in which she had always intended to nurture and raise him, although cruel time had prevented her from doing so. She also added that, just as she was praying to God with all her heart that He would forgive the Queen of England for her offence, so he should forget it all, love her, and obey her as if she were his own mother. She finally gestured with her hand, and with her voice she

che dovessero andare per parte sua a ritrovare il Re suo figliolo il quale haveria suplito a quanto ella non poteva, et in questa occasione voltata la faccia, protestò altamente al populo chiamando Iddio in testimonio, che mai ne in fatti ne in parlamento haveva ne cospirato, ne consentito a cospirazione alcuna contro la Regina d'Inghilterra pregando Iddio a non le perdonar le sue colpe se mentiva, poi rivoltatasi al sudetto Mastro di Casa li disse che facesse le sue raccomandationi a suo figliolo et che lo pregasse da parte sua a rimettersi nella Santa Chiesa Cattolica et Romana, nella quale ella haveva sempre avuto intentione di nutrirlo et allevarlo se bene la malignità de tempi l'havevano impedita et che nel resto si come ella pregava Iddio di buon core a perdonar alla Regina d'Inghilterra l'offesa ch'a lei faceva, così egli scordasse il tutto, l'amasse, rispettasse, et obedisse come se li fusse madre, dandogli in ultimo con il segno della mano et con al voce, dicendo In nomine patris, la sua beneditione per portarli; poi messasi a ginocchi sopra un gran cossino di velluto cremesino disse il Credo ad alta voce rendendo testimonio della fede nella quale moriva, et fece una confessione generale delle sue colpe con molte orationi che

said, "in the name of the Father," the blessing to be brought to him. Then, she kneeled on a large cushion of crimson velvet and recited the Creed aloud, as a testimony of the faith in which she would be dying, and made a general confession of her sins with many prayers in Latin, praying every time that her servants would pray to God to give her strength. When the Executioner approached to position her, with the same imperiousness as earlier she rejected him before he'd dared touch her, commanding him not to execute his duty until she had signalled him to. And when the gentleman told her that time was running out, she turned to one of her ladies and called upon her to come blindfold her and adjust the collar of her dress. The woman had to be dragged up to the stage, for she did not want to go there, and since her hands were shaking, the Queen helped her out with her own. Once she had been blindfolded and her neck adjusted, she turned to her people and bid them one last farewell. She kneeled again with her hands clasped and signalled to the Executioner that he could perform his duty, and he cut off her head with an axe in two blows. Then, he lifted it from the ugly blood and showed it to the

disse in latino, pregando ogni qual volta la sua famiglia di pregar Iddio per la sua fermezza: et avvicinandosi il Boia per accomodarla, con il medesimo Imperio di prima lo ributtò senza che ardisse toccarla, comandandogli di non eseguir l'officio suo, se prima ella non glie ne faceva segno. Et dicendoli il Milort che l'hora passava, ella voltatasi ad una delle sue donne la chiamò che li venisse a bendar gl'occhi et accomodar il colare della vesta, che bisognò che fusse strassinata sopra il palco, che non vi voleva andare, et tremandogli la mano, ella medesima con le sue proprie l'aiutava. Bendati gli occhi et accomodato il collo rivoltatasi a suoi li disse l'ultimo A Dio; et tornatasi a metter in genocchion con le man gionte fece segno al Boia di far l'officio suo; il qual con una Cetta in doi colpi li mozzò la testa che poi levata dalla bruttura del sangue fu messa alla vista del populo, che era fuori, sopra una fenestra della sala sopra un cussino di velluto, dove stata un mezzo quarto d'hora dopo che le sue genti furono di novo messe prigioni, et il corpo aperto et imbalsamato. Et in Londra per 24 hore sonorno le campane, tirorno artegliaria et fecero fuochi segno di allegrezza. Morte o per dir meglio martirio molto

people who were outside, by placing it on a velvet cushion in one of the hall's windows, where it remained for a half quarter of an hour after her people were brought back to prison and the body was opened and embalmed. And the bells rang in London for twenty-four hours, the artillery fired, and fireworks were set off as a sign of joy. Her death, or rather, her most lamentable martyrdom brought great sadness to this court, for the memory is still fresh of when she was Queen of France; and the King, Queen, and nobles bear this pain. This is what I thought to write to Your Lordship, whose hands I kiss through my brother, Fabrizio. May the Lord have care of you and may you prosper, along with Sig. Carlo, Sig. Andrea, and Lady Lucrezia and all the children.

compassionevole, et che in questa Corte ha messo grandissima mestizia, per esser frescha anco la memoria quando vi era Regina di Francia, et il Re et Regina con tutta la nobiltà ne portano il dolo: che è quanto mi è parso di scrivere a V.S. alla quale con il Sig. Fabritio mio fratello che si porta benissimo bacio le mani, che il Signor la conservi et prosperi con il Sig. Carlo, Sig. Andrea et Signora Lucretia et tutti li putini.

Paris, 14 March 1587

You Lordship's Son and Affectionate Servant,
Sartorio Loschi

Di Parigi il di 14 Marzo 1587
Di V.S.
Come Figliuolo et Servitore Affezionatiss.
Sartorio Loscho

Bibliography

Manuscript and Printed editions of *La reina di Scotia*

Della Valle, Federico. *Maria la reina*. Biblioteca Civica "Angelo Mai" di Bergamo, Ms. MM166.

– *Maria la reina*. Biblioteca Nazionale di Napoli, Ms. XIII E 2.

– *La reina di Scotia*. Milan: Heredi di Melchior Malatesta, 1628.

– *La reina di Scotia*, ed. Benedetto Croce. Bologna: Zanichelli, 1930.

– *Tutte le opere*, ed. Pietro Cazzani. Milan: Mondadori, 1955.

– *Tragedie*, ed. Andrea Gareffi. Milan: Mursia, 1988.

– *Opere*, ed. Maria Gabriella Stassi. Turin: UTET, 1995.

– *Opere*, ed. Matteo Durante. Messina: Sicania, 2005.

Italian Dramatic Works and Operas on Mary Queen of Scots

Anonymous. *Maria Stuarda a Dombar*. Milan: Placido Maria Visaj, 1829.

Alfieri, Vittorio. *Maria Stuarda*. Paris: Didot, 1789.

Brenna, Amato. *David Rizio, ossia la giovinezza di Maria Stuarda*. Florence: Angelo Romei, 1856.

Canepa, Luigi. *David Rizio*. Libretto by Enrico Costa. Milan, 1871

Capecelatro, Vincenzo. *David Riccio*. Libretto by Andrea Maffei. Milan: Ricordi, 1850.

Caracciolo, Mariano. *La morte di Maria Stuarda*. Palermo: Spampinato, 1835.

Carlini, Luigi. *Maria Stuarda, Regina di Scozia*. Palermo, 1818.

Casella, Pietro. *Maria Stuarda, Regina di Scozia*. Libretto by Francesco Gonella. Florence: Giuseppe Carnevale, 1812.

Castronovo, Francesco. *Maria Stuarda*. Turin: Libreria Salesiana, 1896.

Celli, Orazio. *La Maria Stuarda Regina di Scotia e d'Inghilterra*. Rome: Michele Ercole, 1665.

Coccia, Carlo. *Maria Stuarda, Regina di Scozia*. London, 1828.

Della Valle. *La reina di Scotia*. Milan: Heredi di Melchior Malatesta, 1628.
Donizetti, Gaetano. *Maria Stuarda*. Libretto by Giuseppe Bardari. Milan: Luigi di Giacomo Parola, 1835.
Federici, Camillo. *Il trionfo dei Carbonari*. Padua, 1802.
Gisberti, Domenico. *La barbarie del caso*. Murano, 1664.
Mercadante, Saverio. *Maria Stuarda, Regina di Scozia*. Bologna: Nobili, 1821.
Paccinelli, Antonio. *I trionfi di morte. Opera tragica*. Perugia: Sebastiano Zecchini, 1670.
Palumbo, Costantino. *Maria Stuarda*. Naples, 1874.
Ruggieri, Carlo. *La reina di Scotia*. Naples: Costantino Vitale, 1604.
Sansone, Anselmo. *Maria Stuarda*. Palermo: Pietro dell'Isola, 1672.
Savaro, Giovanni Francesco. *Maria Stuarda*. Bologna: Giacomo Monti, 1663.
Skinner, Florence Marian (F.M. Stresa). *La regina di Scozia*. (Turin, 1883).

Selected Scholarly Works on Mary Queen of Scots and Her Times

Alford, Stephen. *The Early Elizabethan Polity: William Cecil and the British Succession Crisis, 1558–1569*. Cambridge: Cambridge University Press, 1998.
Baldwin Smith, Lacey. *Treason in Tudor England: Politics and Paranoia*. Princeton: Princeton University Press, 1986.
Basing, Patricia. "Robert Beale and the Queen of Scots." *British Library Journal* 20, no. 1 (1994).
Burns, James Henderson. *The True Law of Kingship: Concepts of Monarchy in Early Modern Scotland*. Oxford: Oxford University Press, 1996.
Carta, Veronica. "Alle origini del mito di Maria Stuarda in Italia." PhD diss, Università degli Studi di Cagliari, 2011.
Collinson, Patrick. *The English Captivity of Mary Queen of Scots*. Sheffield: Sheffield History Pamphlets, 1987.
Cowan, Ian Borthwick. *The Enigma of Mary Stuart*. London: Gollancz, 1971.
Croft, Pauline. *King James*. New York: Palgrave Macmillan, 2003.
Davidson, Peter. "The Casket Sonnets: New Evidence Concerning Mary Queen of Scots." *History Scotland Magazine* (Winter 2001): 28–34.
Diggle, Henry Frederick. *The Casket Letters of Mary Stuart: A Study in Fraud and Forgery; A Vindication of the Queen*. Harrogate: Ackrill, 1960.
Donaldson, Gordon. *The First Trial of Mary Queen of Scots*. New York: Stein and Day, 1969.
Erskine, Caroline, and Roger A. Mason, eds. *George Buchanan: Political Thought in Early Modern Britain and Europe*. Farnham: Ashgate, 2012.
Guy, John. *Elizabeth: The Forgotten Years*. London: Penguin, 2017.
– *My Heart Is My Own: The Life of Mary Queen of Scots*. London: Fourth Estate, 2009.
– *The Reign of Elizabeth I: Court and Culture in the Last Decade*. Cambridge: Cambridge University Press, 1995.

Hopkins, Lisa. *Writing Renaissance Queens: Texts by and About Elizabeth I and Mary, Queen of Scots*. Newark: University of Delaware Press, 2002.

Hunt, Alice, and Anna Whitelock. *Tudor Queenship: The Reigns of Mary and Elizabeth*. New York: Palgrave Macmillan, 2010.

Jansen, Sharon L. *The Monstrous Regiment of Women: Female Rulers in Early Modern Europe*. New York: Palgrave Macmillan, 2002.

Kantorowicz, Ernst H. *The King's Two Bodies: A Study in Medieval Political Theology*. Princeton: Princeton University Press, 1957.

Lewis, Jayne Elizabeth. *Mary Queen of Scots: Romance and Nation*. New York: Routledge, 1998.

– *The Trial of Mary Queen of Scots: A Brief History with Documents*. New York: Bedford/St. Martin's Press, 1999.

Labanoff, Alexandre, ed. *Lettres, instructions et mémoires de Marie Stuart, Reine d'Écosse, 6*. London: Charles Dolman, 1844.

Merriman, Marcus. *The Rough Wooings: Mary Queen of Scots, 1542–1551*. East Linton: Tuckwell, 2000.

Muhlstein, Anka. *Elizabeth I and Mary Stuart: The Perils of Marriage*. London: Haus Publishing, 2007.

Phillips, James Emerson. *Images of a Queen: Mary Stuart in Sixteenth-Century Literature*. Berkeley: University of California Press, 1984.

Rossi, *La cultura inglese a Milano e in Lombardia nel Seicento e nel Settecento*. Bari: Adriatica, 1970.

Russo, Stephanie. *The Afterlife of Anne Boleyn: Representations of Anne Boleyn in Fiction and on the Screen*. New York: Palgrave Macmillan, 2020.

Shephard, Amanda. *Gender and Authority in Sixteenth-Century England: The Knox Debate*. Keele: Ryburn, 1994.

Staines, John. *The Tragic Histories of Mary Queen of Scots: Rhetoric, Passions, and Political Literature, 1560–1690*. Farnham: Ashgate, 2009.

Walton, Kristen P. *Catholic Queen, Protestant Patriarchy, Mary, Queen of Scots and the Politics of Gender and Religion*. New York: Palgrave Macmillan, 2007.

Watkins, John. "'Out of her Ashes May a Second Phoenix Rise': James I and the Legacy of Elizabethan Anti-Catholicism," in *Catholicism and Anti-Catholicism in Early Modern English Texts*, ed. Arthur F. Marotti. New York: Palgrave Macmillan, 1999.

Weir, Alison. *Mary Queen of Scots and the Murder of Lord Darnley*. New York: Ballantine Books, 2009.

Wilkinson, Alexander. *Mary Queen of Scots and French Public Opinion, 1542–1600*. New York: Palgrave Macmillan, 2004.

Wormald, Jenny. *Mary Queen of Scots: A Study in Failure*. London: Philip, 1988.

Wyatt, Michael. *The Italian Encounter with Tudor England: A Cultural Politics of Translation*. Cambridge: Cambridge University Press, 2005.

Selected Scholarly Works on Federico Della Valle and Seventeenth-Century Tragedies

Baldis, Bruno. "Di una nuova redazione manoscritta della tragedia *La Reina di Scotia* di Federico Della Valle." *Aevum* 26, no. 4 (1952).

Cascetta, Annamaria, and Roberta Carpani, eds. *La scena della gloria: Drammaturgia e spettacolo a Milano in età spagnola*. Milan: Vita e pensiero, 1995.

Cerbo, Anna. "Una *Reina di Scotia* poco nota." *Annali dell'Istituto Universitario Orientale* (1984): 395–431.

Colombo, Cesare. "Federico Della Valle a Milano." *Italia Medioevale e Umanistica* 9 (1966): 477–85.

Croce, Benedetto (Gustave Colline). "Ancora della *Reina di Scotia* di Federigo Della Valle." *La critica* 34 (1936).

– "Il tema Maria Stuarda." *Problemi di estetica e contributi alla storia dell'estetica italiana*. Rome-Bari: Laterza, 1954.

– "Le tragedie di Federico Della Valle di Asti," *Nuovi saggi sulla letteratura italiana del Seicento*. Bari: Laterza, 1931.

– "Notizie di opere letterarie italiane su Maria Stuarda." *Rassegna pugliese di arti e lettere* 2 (September 1885).

– "Storia dell'età barocca in Italia." *Scritti di storia letteraria e politica*. Rome-Bari: Laterza, 1924.

Croce, Franco. *Federico Della Valle*. Florence: La Nuova Italia, 1965.

Dalla Valle, Daniela. "Il tema della fortuna nella tragedia italiana rinascimentale e barocca." *Italica* 44, no. 2 (1967): 180–208.

Dalla Valle, Daniela, and Monica Pavesio, eds. *Due storie inglesi, due miti europei: Maria Stuarda e il Conte di Essex sulle scene teatrali*. Alessandria: Edizioni dell'Orso, 2006.

Durante, Matteo. "La Maria Stuarda dellavalliana." *In assenza del re: Le reggenti dal XIV al XVII secolo (Piemonte ed Europa)*, ed. Franca Varallo. Florence: Olshki, 2008.

– "Per una biografia culturale." Federico Della Valle, *Opere*, vol. 1, ed. Matteo Durante. Messina: Sicania, 2005.

– "La prima redazione della *Reina di Scotia* di Federico Della Valle: Bergamo, Biblioteca Civica, ms. MM 166." *Siculorum Gymnasium* 34, no. 2 (1981).

– *Restauri dellavalliani*. Catania: Università di Catania, 1983.

Filosa, Carlo. "Contributo allo studio della biografia di Federico Della Valle." *Giornale storico della letteratura italiana* 17 (1938): 161–210.

Franchi, Saverio. *Drammaturgia romana: Repertorio bibliografico cronologico dei testi drammatici pubblicati a Roma e nel Lazio, Secolo XVII*. Rome: Edizioni di Storia e Letteratura, 1988.

Gerato, Erasmo G. "Un'anima traviata: *La Reina di Scotia* di Federico Della Valle." *Neuphilologische Mitteilungen* 81, no. 1 (1980): 7–14.

Getto, Giovanni. "Il teatro barocco di Federico Della Valle." *Il Verri* 2 (1958): 14–52.

Jannaco, Carmine, and Martino Capuci. *Storia letteraria d'Italia: Il Seicento.* Milan: Vallardi, 1973.

Kipka, Karl. *Maria Stuart im Drama des Weltliteratur: Vornehmlich Des 17. Und 18. Jahrhunderts. Ein Beitrag Zur Vergleichenden Literaturgeschichte.* Leipzig: Metzler, 1907.

Mancini, Albert N., and Glenn Palen Pierce. *Seventeenth Century Italian Poets and Dramatists.* Detroit: Gale Cengage Learning, 2008.

Mercuri, Roberto. "La *Reina di Scotia* di Federico della Valle e la forma della tragedia gesuitica." *Calibano* 4 (1979): 142–61.

Olivari, Edy. "Maria Stuarda nel teatro del Seicento / Marie Stuart dans le théâtre du XVIIe siècle." PhD sissertation, Università degli Studi di Torino / Université de Savoie, 2007.

Romei, Giovanna. "Della Valle, Federico." In *Dizionario Biografico degli Italiani,* vol. 37. Rome: Istituto della Enciclopedia Italiana, 1989.

Sanguineti White, Laura. *Dal detto alla figura: Le tragedie di Federico Della Valle.* Florence: Olshki, 1992.

Strappini, Lucia. "Esercizi dello spirito: qualche nota sul teatro dei Gesuiti tra fine Cinquecento e metà Seicento." In *Paolo Segneri: Un classico della tradizione cristiana,* ed. Rocco Paternostro and Andrea Fedi. Stony Brook: Forum Italicum, 1999.

Trombatore, Gaetano. "Le tragedie di Federico Della Valle." In *Saggi critici.* Florence: La Nuova Italia, 1955.

Villani, Stefano. "From Mary Queen of Scots to the Scottish Capuchins: Scotland as a Symbol of Protestant Persecution in Seventeenth-Century Italian Literature." *Innes Review* 64, no. 2 (2013): 100–19.

Zanlonghi, Giovanna. *Teatri di formazione: Actio, parola e immagine nella scena gesuitica del Sei-Settecento a Milano.* Milan: Vita e Pensiero, 2002.

Index